Ann Bowen and John Pallister

geography 360°

Core Book 1

www.heinemann.co.uk
✓ Free online support
✓ Useful weblinks
✓ 24 hour online ordering

01865 888058

Heine
Inspiring

An

D0987758

000000009979

Heinemann Educational Publishers
Halley Court, Jordan Hill, Oxford OX2 8EJ
Part of Harcourt Education

Heinemann is the registered trademark of
Harcourt Education Limited

© Ann Bowen, John Pallister, 2004

First published 2004

09 08 07 06 05 04
10 9 8 7 6 5 4 3 2 1

British Library Cataloguing in Publication Data is available
from the British Library on request.

ISBN 0 435 35643 7

Copyright notice

All rights reserved. No part of this publication may be reproduced in any form or by any
means (including photocopying or storing it in any medium by electronic means and whether
or not transiently or incidentally to some other use of this publication) without the written
permission of the copyright owner, except in accordance with the provisions of the Copyright,
Designs and Patents Act 1988 or under the terms of a licence issued by the Copyright
Licensing Agency, 90 Tottenham Court Road, London W1T 4LP. Applications for the copyright
owner's written permission should be addressed to the publisher.

Edited by Caroline Hannan
Designed by hicksdesign and typeset and illustrated by Hardlines Ltd
Original illustrations © Harcourt Education Limited, 2003
Printed and bound in Italy by Printer Trento S.r.l
Cover photo: © Getty images
Picture research by Beatrice Ray

Acknowledgements

Maps and extracts

All OS maps reproduced from Ordnance Survey mapping with the permission of Her
Majesty's Stationery Office, © Crown copyright, Licence no. 10000230. Source B, page 41
produced by the Office for National Statistics website 2001. Source D, page 75 logos with
permission from Nike™, Reebok™, Adidas™ and New Balance™. Source D, page 87
'Highland Fling' adapted from an article by Kirsty Scott in The Guardian, 25 July 2002.

Photos

Pages 15, 102, 90: Alamy. Page 113, Barking Council. Page 103, Bluewater shopping
centre. Page 7, Caroline Hannan. Page 94, Collections. Page 13, Corbis. Page 28, Durham
Country Council. Page 47, Empics. Page 74, Getty. Page 60, Getty News and Sport. Page
75, Graeme Peacock. Page 76, Harcourt / Corbis. Page 52, Lowry / Tate Gallery / Courtesy
of Carol Lowry. Page 87, Murdo McLeod. Page 22, National Trust. Page 80, Rex. Page 63,
Rex/Dave Bartruff. Page 105, Sainsburys. Page 5, Science Photo Library. Page 95, Topham.
Page 95, Topham/Joe Sohm. Pages 29 and 96 kindly supplied by author Ann Bowen. All
other pages with photographs kindly supplied by the author John Pallister.

Every effort has been made to contact copyright holders of material reproduced in this book.
omissions will be rectified in subsequent printings if notice is given to the publishers.

Websites
On pages where you are
asked to go to
www.heinemann.co.uk/hotli
nks to complete a task or
download information,
please insert the code
6437P at the website.

Contents

» 1   What is geography all about?

Can you pick out the British Isles on this satellite view of part of the Earth? The main area of study in geography is the Earth's surface.

Learning objectives

What are you going to learn about in this chapter?

> The difference between physical and human geography
> The different landscapes on the Earth's surface
> How to divide up the world for easier study
> How to find a place on a map using latitude and longitude

How are physical and human geography different?

>> **Understanding how physical and human geography are different**
>> **Learning how to draw a labelled sketch from a photograph**

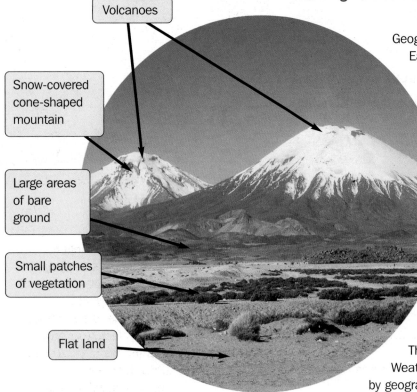

Volcanoes

Snow-covered cone-shaped mountain

Large areas of bare ground

Small patches of vegetation

Flat land

A **Volcanoes in Chile in South America**

Geography is the study of places and people on the Earth's surface. To be a good geographer, you need to be good at observing **landscapes**.

Look at photograph **A**. Adding labels to a photograph is one way of describing what you can observe.

The labels show the **physical** features of this landscape. A volcano is an example of a physical feature. It is a natural feature, not something made by people. When molten **lava** from underground pours out on to the Earth's surface, it forms volcanoes. After a long time, a cone-shaped mountain is built.

The snow on the top of the volcano in photograph **A** has come from the **atmosphere**. The **weather** on mountain tops is often cold. Weather is another natural feature that is studied by geographers. Notice that there are few signs of people living in this area. Therefore, there are no features of **human geography** worth labelling on photograph **A**.

Key words

Atmosphere – layer of air surrounding the Earth's surface

Human geography – changes to the Earth's surface made by people

Landscape – the natural scenery of an area and what it looks like

Lava – molten material that flows out of a volcano and cools into rock

Physical geography – natural features on the Earth's surface

Weather – outdoor conditions at a particular time: hot or cold, clear or cloudy, wet or dry, windy or calm

B **Soufriere Hills volcano, Montserrat**

Photograph **B** shows an active volcano. Ash and dust are being forced out of its crater. How has the volcano affected the area around it? People living in the houses you can see were forced to flee several years ago.

This volcano on the Caribbean island of Montserrat has erupted almost continuously since 1995. Check to see if it is still active by clicking on www.heinemann.co.uk/hotlinks and inserting express code **6437P**.

Now look at photograph **C**. This was taken in Delhi, a city in India. The scene could not be more different. Buildings, roads, traffic and people are everywhere. Indeed, can you see any physical features at all on this photograph?

 Street scene in Delhi, India

Activities

1   Look at photograph **C**.

   a) What can you see? Describe the human features. Are there any physical (natural) features shown? The more you can observe and write, the better your answer will be.

   b) Is this street scene anything like the one in your nearest town or city? Complete a table of similarities and differences like the one below.

Similarities	Differences

2   Look at photograph **D**.

   a) Name *two* physical features shown.

   b) Name *two* human features shown.

3   a) Draw a labelled sketch of either photograph **B** or photograph **D**. (See the SKILLS box for how to do this.)

   b) Compare your sketch with those of your neighbours in the class. Mark each of them out of 10. Use the following guide to marking:

   • Amount of detail shown – up to 4 marks

   • Appearance and neatness – up to 2 marks

   • Number of different labels – up to 4 marks.

   Work out a total out of 10.

   c) Do any of the sketches deserve a higher mark than your own? Give reasons for your answer.

   d) What *two* things would improve your own sketch?

SKILLS

How to draw a labelled sketch from a photograph

1 Make a frame the same size as the photograph.

2 In the frame, draw or trace the main features shown.

3 Label the main physical and human features.

4 Give your sketch a title.

For more help see page 125 of *SKILLS in geography*.

 Steamboat Springs, Colorado, USA

The Earth's different landscapes

>> Learning about the Earth's tropical, temperate and polar zones
>> Looking at how the Earth's zones affect the weather

The Earth's surface can be divided into **tropical**, **temperate** and **polar** zones. (See diagram **A**.)

B Tropical rainforest in Malaysia, Asia

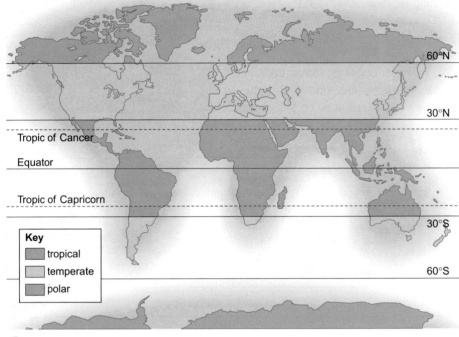

A The Earth's surface split into three zones

C Hot desert in northern Chile, South America

TROPICAL ZONE

In the tropics it is always hot. Average daily temperatures are about 30°C. The sun shines from high in the sky.

Around the **Equator**, heavy rain falls all year. Strong sunlight and high rainfall give perfect conditions for plants to grow. Trees and plants grow faster, taller and in greater numbers than anywhere else on the Earth's surface. Look at the rainforest in photograph **B**. Rainforest grows near the Equator. The natural vegetation is the densest and most varied on the Earth's surface.

Around the tropics of **Cancer** and **Capricorn**, the weather is different. It is still hot every day, but it rains less. Here large areas of hot **desert** are found, such as the Sahara in Africa – the world's largest desert. In a desert, less than 250 mm of rain falls during the year. The desert surface in photograph **C** is mainly bare rock, stones and sand.

POLAR ZONE

D Ice in Greenland

Polar lands are cold. Ninety per cent of Greenland is covered by an ice sheet (see **D**). The sun shines from low in the sky; there is no sunlight at all in midwinter. Temperatures fall as low as −50°C and large areas are covered by ice and snow.

TEMPERATE ZONE

Temperate lands lie between the tropical and polar zones. They can be hot in summer, but are not hot all year. This makes them different from the tropics. They can be cold in winter, but the cold lasts for only a few months. This makes them different from polar regions.

The UK is located in temperate lands. How would you describe the UK's weather? Hot or cold? Wet or dry? Cloudy or sunny? What do you think about the weather in the UK? Does anyone live in the UK because of its weather?

E Farming on the North York Moors, England

Activities

(S) 📄

1 Key words – mix and match

First copy the list of key words. Then write the correct definition next to each key word.

Key words:	Definitions:
Tropic of Cancer	Cold lands north and south of 60°
Tropic of Capricorn	Line of latitude 23½° north of the Equator
Equator	Areas up to 23½° north and south of the Equator
Polar regions	Lands between hot tropical and cold polar regions
Temperate regions	Line of latitude 23½° south of the Equator
Tropics	0° line of latitude around the middle of the Earth

2
a) Look at photograph **E**.

  (i) Write down *two* things that show it is a farming area.

  (ii) Write down the other activity shown in the photograph.

b) Write down what you can see in photograph **C** that shows that it is drier and hotter near the tropics than in the UK.

c) Write down what you can see in photograph **D** that shows it is colder in polar lands than in the UK.

3 Types of work and leisure activities

a) Read the list of activities below. Do you think that the UK's weather is good or bad for each of these?

*Gardening   Farming   Taking seaside holidays
Playing cricket   Driving a lorry*

b) Copy the table below. Complete the two rows that have been started.

Work/activity	Good	Bad
Driving a lorry	Dry, clear skies – make driving safer	
Farming		Cold in winter – crops cannot grow

c) Choose two more activities from the list above to fill in two more rows.

4
a) What is your weather like today?

b) What do you like *most* and *least* about weather in the UK?

c) Check with others in the class to find out whether their likes and dislikes are the same as yours.

d) Would you prefer to live in the tropics or in polar lands? Or are you happy living in a temperate land? Give *three* reasons for your answer.

How can the world be divided up?

>> **Understanding how geographers divide the world up**

>> **Practising your atlas skills**

The world is a big place. To make it easier to study, geographers divide it up in different ways.

One way is to split the world into **northern** and **southern hemispheres**. Look at diagram **A**. The **Equator** is the imaginary line between the two hemispheres. The UK is in the northern hemisphere. Australia is a country in the southern hemisphere.

Does it make any difference which hemisphere a person lives in? Water swirls anti-clockwise before going down the plug hole in the northern hemisphere; in the southern hemisphere it goes clockwise. That is one difference, but it is not important to a geographer. What is important is that the seasons are different. Summer in the southern hemisphere is December, January and February. During these months the sun is overhead south of the Equator, so that is the hot time of year. This is when summer sports like cricket are played in Australia. Look at photograph **B**. This test match was played in November. What was the season?

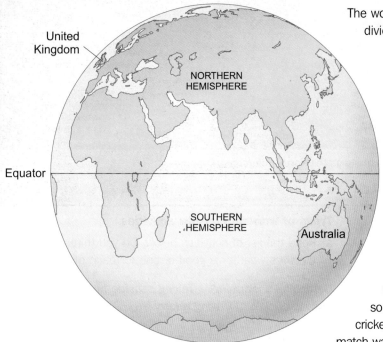

A Northern and southern hemispheres

B Test match between Australia and England in Brisbane, Australia

Another way of dividing up the world is into land and water (map **C**). Seventy per cent of the Earth's surface is covered by **oceans** and seas. Less than one-third of the Earth's surface is left for people to live on.

The Earth's land surface is divided into seven **continents**. Asia covers the largest area. More people live in Asia than in all the other continents added together. Only six of the seven continents are inhabited. No one lives permanently in Antarctica, although there are a few bases used by scientists. Ice, snow and the bitter cold stop people from living there but not penguins (photograph **D**).

Key words

Continent – area of land covering a large area of the Earth's surface

Equator – the imaginary line dividing the northern from the southern hemisphere

Hemisphere – one half of the Earth

Northern hemisphere – that half of the Earth north of the Equator

Ocean – great body of water surrounding the Earth's land masses

Southern hemisphere – that half of the Earth south of the Equator

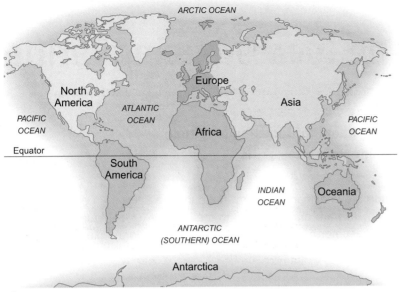

C The Earth's oceans and continents

However, the Arctic is different. It is an ocean, not a continent. There is no land at the North Pole. There is plenty of ice but only the sea surface is frozen and there is water below the ice.

D Hope Bay, Antarctica

Activities

1 Seasons in the UK

Winter	December–February
Spring	March–May
Summer	June–August
Autumn	September–November

Make another box like this with the title **Seasons in Australia** and fill it in with the correct months.

2 Write out and complete the following sentences.

a) The three northern hemisphere continents are_____

b) The continents with most or all of their land in the southern hemisphere are _____

c) The continent split in half by the Equator is _____

d) The continent without any people living there all the time is _____

3 a) Make a frame and draw a sketch of photograph **D** (see SKILLS, page 7 for how to do this). Add labels to describe what can be seen.

b) A wilderness is defined by geographers as 'an area untouched by humans, where the landscape is dominated by natural (physical) features'.
Write down what you can see on photograph **D** that shows Antarctica is a wilderness.

4 In an atlas, find a world map of countries.

a) Name the countries that the Equator passes through.

b) What is the total number?

c) There are about 180 countries in the world. The Equator passes through only a small number of them. Why? (Hint – look at the distribution of land and water.)

SKILLS

How to use an atlas 1
Countries of the world
1 Find the Contents page in the front of your atlas.
2 Look for the heading *World*.
3 Then search for a political map.
A political map shows country names, boundaries and major cities.

For more help see page 121 of *SKILLS in geography*.

How can places be located using latitude and longitude?

>> **Learning about latitude and longitude**
>> **Practising your atlas skills**

Key words

Latitude – is measured in degrees *north* or *south* of the Equator
Longitude – is measured in degrees *east* or *west* of the Greenwich meridian line
Greenwich meridian – the 0° line of longitude that passes through Greenwich in London

Lines of **latitude** are imaginary lines drawn around the Earth from east to west (see diagram **A**). They are drawn parallel to the Equator (0°). Latitude is measured in degrees north or south of the Equator. The North Pole is 90°N and the South Pole is 90°S.

Lines of **longitude** are imaginary lines drawn from north to south. They go from the North Pole to the South Pole. The 0° line of longitude passes through Greenwich in London. This is why it is called the **Greenwich meridian**. All the other lines of longitude are numbered in degrees east or west of the Greenwich line, up to 180°E and 180°W. The 180° line of longitude passes through the Pacific Ocean, east of New Zealand.

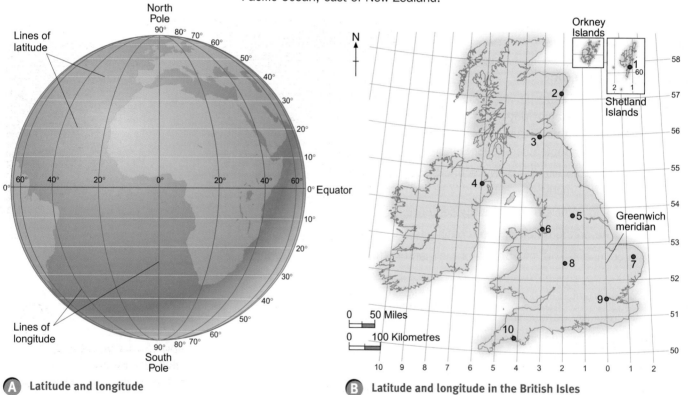

A Latitude and longitude

B Latitude and longitude in the British Isles

There are 360° of longitude (180°E plus 180°W). Every 24 hours the Earth spins through 360°. The world is divided into 24 time zones based on longitude. For every 15° of longitude the time difference is one hour. Can you work out why it is 15°?

One degree of latitude is about 110 kilometres (70 miles). Latitude 50°N passes through the southern tip of Cornwall. Latitude 60°N passes through the Shetland Islands. Therefore, the UK extends through 10 degrees of latitude. This makes it about 1100 kilometres (700 miles) long 'as the crow flies' (in a straight line) (see map **B**).

	Latitude	Longitude
Greenwich	51°28′N	0°00′
Aberdeen	57°09′N	2°09′W
Belfast	54°37′N	5°56′W
Birmingham	52°25′N	1°55′W
Edinburgh	55°55′N	3°10′W
Leeds	53°45′N	1°30′W
Lerwick	60°09′N	1°10′W
Liverpool	53°25′N	3°00′W
Norwich	52°38′N	1°19′E
Plymouth	50°25′N	4°05′W

C Latitudes and longitudes of ten places in the UK

One degree of latitude *or* longitude is divided into 60 minutes (60′).

Minutes allow places to be located more exactly. If you know both the latitude and longitude of a place, you can locate any place in the world.

Highest mountain
Mount Everest (8848 m)
28°03′N 87°07′E

Lowest land
Around the Dead Sea (395 m below sea level)
In the centre –
31°30′N 35°30′E

Longest river
Nile (6690 km (4180 miles))
At the sea – 31°06′N 30°10′E

Driest place
In the Atacama desert (rainfall per year – nil)
24°00′S 69°20′W

Highest waterfall
Angel Falls (1000 m)
5°57′N 62°30′W

Largest island
Greenland (over 2 million km²)
In the centre – 70°00′N 40°W

Largest river
Amazon (20 per cent of all river water in the world)
At the sea – 0°00′ 50°00′W

Wettest place
Cherrapunji (rainfall per year – 10 798 mm, compared with 610 mm in London)
25°17′N 91°47′E

D The world's record-breaking features

E Mount Everest, the highest mountain

F Angel Falls, the highest waterfall

Activities

1 a) Using Table **C**, write down the names of the places in the UK marked 1 to 10 on map **B**.

b) Write down which of the ten places is furthest:

(i) south (ii) north (iii) east (iv) west.

c) In what way is the location of Norwich different from that of all the other places?

2 a) On an outline map of the world, mark, name and label the eight places named in Box **D**.

b) Label the country or countries and continents in which each of the eight places is located.

3 Work in groups and use an atlas (see also SKILLS: Finding a place). Each group researches information about a different place in Box **D**, and then makes a short presentation to everyone else. Try to find out at least five pieces of information. For example, who lives there? Do people visit there? You could include photos or maps to illustrate your presentation.

SKILLS

How to use an atlas 2
Finding a place

1 Turn to the Index at the back of your atlas.

2 Places are named in *alphabetical order*.

3 The *page* for the map you need is given first.

4 Its *square* is given second.

5 Next its *latitude* is stated, and then its *longitude*.

For more help see page 121 of *SKILLS in geography*.

What is geography all about?

Do you now know the difference between physical and human geography?

1 a) How many of the four labels on photograph **A** show features of physical geography?

  b) Can you add another physical geography label?

  c) Can you add another human geography label?

Egyptian village

House being made larger

Sailing boat

River Nile

A The Nile Valley in southern Egypt

Do you know about some of the different landscapes in the world?

2 a) Write about what you can see on photograph **B**, which shows another landscape in the tropics.

  b) Look back at photographs **B** and **C** on page 8. State *two* ways in which the landscape in **B** on *this* page is different from the landscapes shown in each of those photographs.

B Savanna lands of East Africa

The world is divided up into oceans and continents. Do you know their names?

3 Look carefully at map **C**.

  a) Name the continents marked A–C.

  b) Name the oceans marked D–F.

Can you find a place on a map using only its latitude and longitude?

4 a) Look at a map of North America. Which tall city is at latitude 40°47′N and longitude 73°58′W?

  b) Look at a map of Australia. Name the city with a famous opera house and bridge at latitude 34°00′S and longitude 151°00′E.

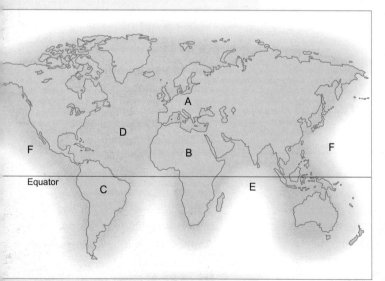

Equator

C Outline map of the world

>> 2   Using Ordnance Survey maps

What are the main features of the landscape shown in the photograph?

Can you spot those same features on the OS map?

Learning objectives

What are you going to learn about in this chapter?

> How to use map symbols

> How to use four- and six-figure grid references

> How to work out distance and direction

> How the height and shape of the land are shown on maps

> How to draw and label a sketch map and a cross-section

> How to investigate settlements on an OS map

A OS map and photograph showing Cuckmere Haven on the south coast of England, scale 1:25 000

© Crown copyright, Licence no. 100000230

Understanding maps

>> Learning what all good maps should have
>> Understanding map symbols

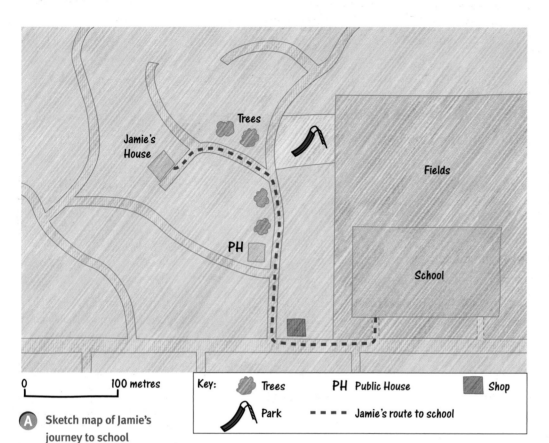

Key: Trees   PH Public House   Shop
Park   - - - - Jamie's route to school

 Sketch map of Jamie's journey to school

How do people learn where places are or what a landscape is like? How do they know how to drive to new places when they go on holiday? Most people would look at a **map**. They might look in a world atlas to find a country or large city. For smaller places and other features they would need more detailed maps. They may even ask a friend to draw a quick sketch map like the one in **A**.

Maps show the features of a landscape as a drawing. They show '**a bird's eye view**', as if the person drawing the map was high above the landscape in a hot-air balloon. Maps would be far too crowded if all the features had to be written on them.

Every map should have:
- a title
- a **north sign**
- a **scale** to show how long things are or how far apart they are
- a frame
- a **key** to show what the different symbols mean.

Symbols are used to show different features of the landscape. The symbols have different characteristics. Some use different colours, others have different shapes, and some are abbreviations of the actual words.

In **B** you can see some of the symbols used on a 1:25 000 Ordnance Survey (OS) map. The map key tells the map reader what the different symbols mean. Try to learn as many of the symbols as you can. It makes reading maps easier and quicker. All 1:25 000 OS maps use the same symbols.

Do you know what all the words in **B** mean, such as a *triangulation pillar*, a *cutting*, or a *coniferous tree*? Use a dictionary to look up any you do not know, and note them down.

Key words

Bird's eye view – a view point from high above the landscape
Key – tells you the meaning of the symbols used on a map
Map – a plan of the landscape
North sign – an arrow that shows the direction of north on a map
Scale – tells you how long things are or how far apart they are
Symbol – a picture or drawing that represents real features on a landscape

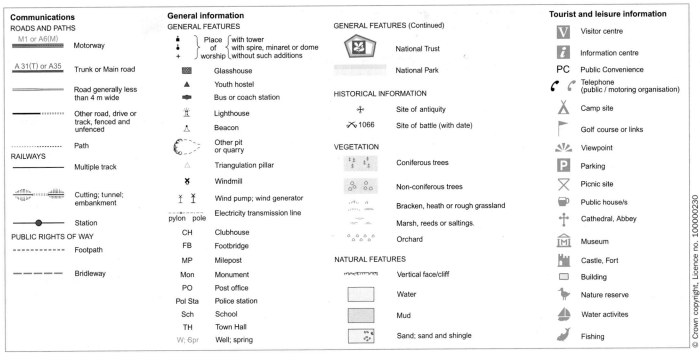

Communications

ROADS AND PATHS

M1 or A6(M)	Motorway
A 31(T) or A35	Trunk or Main road
	Road generally less than 4 m wide
	Other road, drive or track, fenced and unfenced
	Path

RAILWAYS

	Multiple track
	Cutting; tunnel; embankment
	Station

PUBLIC RIGHTS OF WAY

| | Footpath |
| | Bridleway |

General information

GENERAL FEATURES

	Place of worship {with tower / with spire, minaret or dome / without such additions}
	Glasshouse
▲	Youth hostel
	Bus or coach station
	Lighthouse
	Beacon
	Other pit or quarry
△	Triangulation pillar
✗	Windmill
	Wind pump; wind generator
pylon pole	Electricity transmission line
CH	Clubhouse
FB	Footbridge
MP	Milepost
Mon	Monument
PO	Post office
Pol Sta	Police station
Sch	School
TH	Town Hall
W; Spr	Well; spring

GENERAL FEATURES (Continued)

| | National Trust |
| | National Park |

HISTORICAL INFORMATION

| ⚚ | Site of antiquity |
| ⚔1066 | Site of battle (with date) |

VEGETATION

	Coniferous trees
	Non-coniferous trees
	Bracken, heath or rough grassland
	Marsh, reeds or saltings.
	Orchard

NATURAL FEATURES

	Vertical face/cliff
	Water
	Mud
	Sand; sand and shingle

Tourist and leisure information

V	Visitor centre
i	Information centre
PC	Public Convenience
✆	Telephone (public / motoring organisation)
⚑	Camp site
	Golf course or links
	Viewpoint
P	Parking
✗	Picnic site
	Public house/s
✝	Cathedral, Abbey
	Museum
	Castle, Fort
	Building
	Nature reserve
	Water activites
	Fishing

© Crown copyright, Licence no. 100000230

B Selected symbols from a 1:25 000 Ordnance Survey map (Explorer series)

Activities

(S) (📄) (A)

1 Cover up **B** and try to guess what the symbols in **C** represent.

Then check **B** to see if you were right.

2 All maps should have five things. Spot which of these five things is missing on **A**.

3 Looking at **D**, use **B** to answer these questions:

a) What do the OS symbols shown in black mean?

b) What do the OS symbols shown in blue mean?

c) What do the OS symbols shown in red mean?

d) What do the OS symbols shown as abbreviations mean?

4 Using **B**, draw and name the following OS symbols. Use the correct colour or write the colour beside your drawing.

a) church with a tower   b) castle   c) railway

d) viewpoint   e) campsite   f) lighthouse

5 a) Test each other on OS symbols. Write down at least *five* questions using the symbols shown in **B**. Some questions should ask for the name of a symbol. The rest should ask for the symbol to be drawn.

b) Work with a partner. Test each other using your questions. How many did you get right?

a) b) c) d)

C

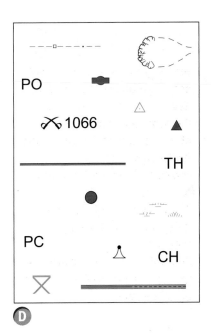
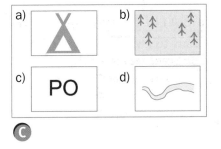

PO   ⚔1066   △   ▲   TH   PC   CH

D

Finding places on an OS map

>> Learning about four-figure grid references
>> Understanding how to find a point inside a map's grid square

Have you noticed the blue lines that form a grid on Ordnance Survey maps? The **grid lines** are always one kilometre apart. A heavier line marks every tenth kilometre. The grid lines (diagram **A**) are numbered around the edge of the map but also at intervals on the map itself. The lines with numbers along the bottom are called **eastings** because they increase in value as you travel from left to right on the map. The lines with numbers up the side are called **northings**. They increase in value as you travel from the bottom to the top of the map. The grid lines make it possible to locate exact points on the map by giving a **grid reference**.

A four-figure grid reference is used to locate a grid square on the map (see the SKILLS 1 box). A grid square shows an area of one square kilometre.

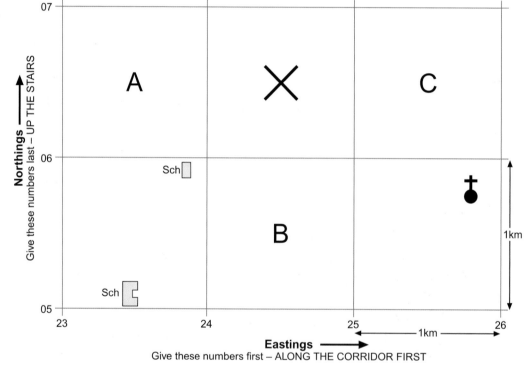

A Four-figure grid references

SKILLS 1

How to give a four-figure grid reference

1 Write down the number of the line that forms the left-hand side of the square – the easting.
2 Write down the number of the line that forms the bottom of the square, the northing.
3 Always write the numbers one after each other – do not add commas, hyphens, brackets or a space.
4 Write the number from along the bottom of the map first, then the number up the side.

Remember this by saying: GO ALONG THE CORRIDOR THEN UP THE STAIRS!

For example, in **A** the four-figure grid reference for grid square X is 2406.

For more help see page 121 of *SKILLS in geography*.

Look at grid square 2305 on **A**. Why would this four-figure grid reference be useless if you wanted to meet your friend at the school?

Did you notice that there are two schools in the grid square? The four-figure grid reference would not be accurate enough. A six-figure grid reference is needed to locate an exact point within a grid square, such as your own house, a church or a post office.

To give a six-figure grid reference, imagine that each grid square is further divided into ten along each side, giving 100 small squares. Each small square shows an area of 10 000 square metres (**B**). (See also SKILLS 2.)

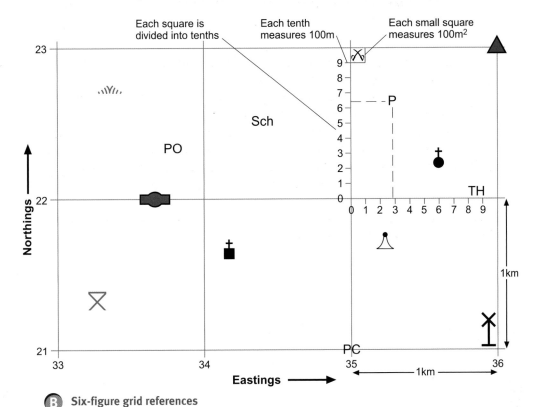

B Six-figure grid references

SKILLS 2

How to give a six-figure grid reference

1 Write down the numbers of the line that forms the left-hand side of the square.

2 Imagine the bottom of the square is divided into tenths (see **B**). Write down the number of tenths the symbol lies along the line.

3 Write down the number of the line that forms the bottom of the square.

4 Imagine the side of the square is divided into tenths. Write down the number of tenths the symbol lies upwards in the square.

In **B** the six-figure grid reference of P is 352226. The six-figure grid reference of ▲ is 360230.

For more help see page 121 of *SKILLS in geography*.

Activities

1 Using the SKILLS 1 box and diagram **A**.

a) Work out the four-figure grid reference for points A, B and C.

b) Draw and name the symbols in grid squares 2305 and 2505.

2 Study **B**. Give the four-figure grid references for the grid squares containing these features.

a) Picnic site   b) Wind pump   c) School

3 Using the SKILLS 2 box and diagram **B**, work out the six-figure grid references for these features.

a) Battlefield   b) Church with a spire   c) Town Hall

4 Using **B**, draw and name the symbols at these six-figure grid references.

a) 344225   b) 352217   c) 350210

5 a) Choose a symbol from **B**. Work out its six-figure map reference.

b) Swap grid references with a partner. Can you find and name the symbols from each other's six-figure grid references?

Key words

Eastings – the lines that increase in value from left to right (west to east) on the map

Grid lines – the blue lines that divide a map into grid squares that measure 1 km squared

Grid reference – used to locate either a grid square (four-figure) or a place within a grid square (six-figure)

Northings – the lines that increase in value from bottom to top (south to north)

How far is it and in which direction?

>> Understanding the points of the compass
>> Learning about scale

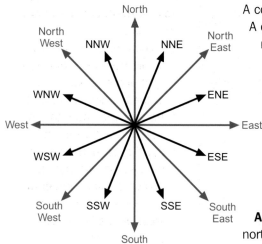

A Points of the compass

A compass has a magnetic needle that swings around until it is pointing north. A compass is used to give directions, and the compass points are very useful in map reading. The four main or **cardinal points** are north, south, east and west (see **A**).

Remember the order they go in by saying: '**N**aughty **E**lephants **S**quirt **W**ater'. Another way is to remember that when north is at the top, you can read WE across. **Ordnance Survey maps are always drawn so that north is at the top of the sheet.**

Between these main points there are NE, SE, NW and SW, giving eight points. Notice how the main points, north or south, are always put first. **A** shows sixteen points of the compass. Look at the point between north and northeast. Notice again how the point in between has been written: NNE. It lies between north and northeast, so N is written first, because it is the main point, followed by NE. It is a good idea to learn these and always use them when talking about **direction** in geography, rather than left, right, top and bottom!

From the farm to the church with a spire is North.

From the farm to the pump is North-East.

From the farm to the Post Office is West.

Can you work out the direction from the farm to the Town Hall?

B How to use a compass

When you give a compass direction, find the starting point and give the direction you need to go in to reach the end point. Study **B** to see some examples.

Planning a walk or working out how far away your friend lives? You need to use the **scale** on the map. The scale tells you how far apart things are or how long they are. The scale is always written on the front cover of an OS map. On an OS map the scale is usually shown in three ways:

- As a linear scale (see **C**)
- As a ratio, for example: 1:25 000 scale
- Written in words: 4 cm to 1 km (on a 1:25 000 map). This means that 4 cm on the map equals 1 km on the ground; in other words, 1 cm on the map = 25 000 cm on the ground.

The other popular scale for a map is 1:50 000. This means that 1 cm on the map represents 0.5 km, or 2 cm = 1 km.

You can use the scale of a map to work out the distance between two points. This can be measured as the distance in a straight line ('as the crow flies') or as a winding distance along a river, roads or paths.

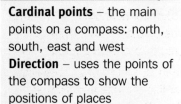

Key words

Cardinal points – the main points on a compass: north, south, east and west

Direction – uses the points of the compass to show the positions of places

Scale – converts the distance on the map to the accurate distance on the ground

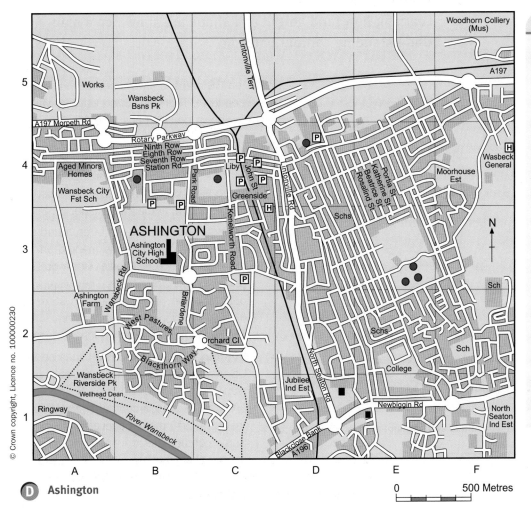

The scale at the top of the page:

1   0   1   2   3

1000   500

metres

kilometres

© Crown copyright, Licence no. 100000230

C OS maps use a linear scale

D Ashington

0   500 Metres

SKILLS

How to measure distances on a map

1 Using a piece of paper or string, accurately mark the start and end point of the distance being measured.
2 Transfer the paper to the linear scale for the map.
3 Put the left-hand mark on the zero and accurately mark the total number of kilometres on the paper.
4 Measure the bit left over using the divided section of the scale. This is in metres.
5 Add the two together to give the final distance measured.
6 Give the units (kilometres or metres) in your answer.

For more help see page 124 of *SKILLS in geography*.

Activities

1 Study map **D**. Find the direction, as the crow flies:

a) from the High School (B3) to the Jubilee Industrial Estate (D1)

b) from the Library (Liby) in C4 to the High School

c) from North Seaton Industrial Estate (F1) to the Hospital (F4).

2 Write the scale for map **D** in words.

3 Use map **D** and the SKILLS box to measure these distances.

a) The length of the River Wansbeck on the map extract.

b) The A196 between the roundabouts in D1 and C5.

4 a) Follow this route and discover the end point.

Start at the roundabout in B3 near the High School. Walk in an easterly direction for about 400 metres and then travel south for about 600 metres. Continue south and then south southeast for a further 750 metres.

b) Someone walking at 6 km per hour takes 10 minutes to walk in a straight line across a 1 km square. Work out how long they would take to walk the route above.

5 Choose two points on map **D**. Write out a route with directions and distances, like the one in activity **4**. Swap routes with a partner. Work out both end points.

Showing the height and shape of the land on an OS map

>> **Learning how land height and shape are shown on a map**
>> **Understanding contour patterns**

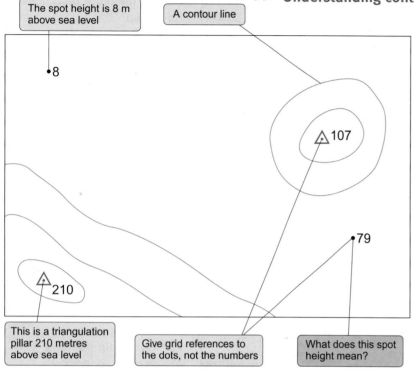

The spot height is 8 m above sea level

A contour line

This is a triangulation pillar 210 metres above sea level

Give grid references to the dots, not the numbers

What does this spot height mean?

A OS maps show spot heights, triangulation pillars and contour lines

Height on OS maps is always shown in metres above sea level. There are three ways in which height is shown on OS maps (see **A**).

- The **spot height** or ground survey height is marked on the map by a black dot with the height in metres alongside (**A**). There is usually nothing to mark a spot height on the actual landscape.

- **Triangulation pillars** are often found on hill tops (**C**). The height is marked on the map by a blue triangle with a dot and the height alongside. They were built for surveyors who used a system of triangles to work out land heights. Triangulation pillars are no longer used.

- **Contour lines** are thin brown lines on an OS map. They join together places at the same height above sea level (**B**). Everywhere along a contour line at 100 metres is 100 metres above sea level. Some contour lines have their height printed along the line.

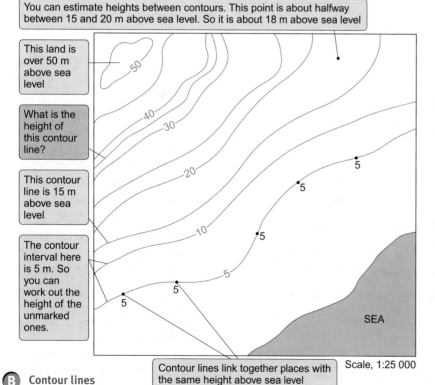

You can estimate heights between contours. This point is about halfway between 15 and 20 m above sea level. So it is about 18 m above sea level

This land is over 50 m above sea level

What is the height of this contour line?

This contour line is 15 m above sea level

The contour interval here is 5 m. So you can work out the height of the unmarked ones.

SEA

Scale, 1:25 000

Contour lines link together places with the same height above sea level

B Contour lines

C A triangulation pillar

On 1:25 000 OS maps contour lines are usually drawn at five-metre intervals. Where the land is very mountainous ten-metre intervals may be used. The difference in height between the contours is called the **contour interval**.

Look at **D** to see how the shape of a hill is linked to how the contours would look on a map.

The pattern made by contour lines on a map tells us about the **relief** of the land. Relief means the height and shape of the land. The steeper the slope, the closer together the contour lines are drawn.

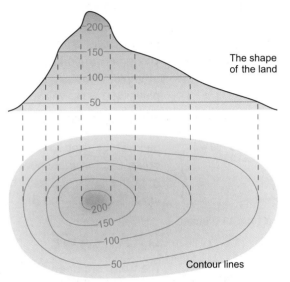

The shape of the land

Contour lines

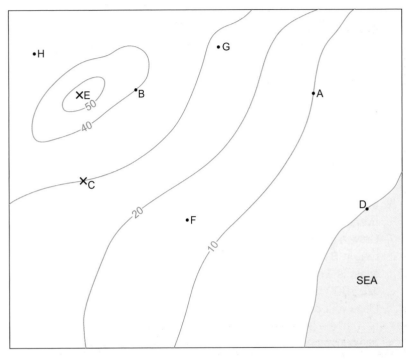

SEA

D How contour lines on a map show the shape of a hill

E Contour intervals

Activities

1. Draw and name the three symbols used to show height on an OS map.

2. Finish this sentence: *A contour line joins together* _____ .

3. a) What is the contour interval on map **E**?

   b) Work out the heights for points A to H on map **E**.

4. Jane sent her friend this on a postcard from her holiday on a Greek island. Draw a map to show the landscape she describes.

> Having a great time, and the resort is stunning. The hotel is right on the beach and faces south. To the west of the hotel there are some steep cliffs and islands just offshore. To the east a pretty river flows through a valley into the sea. Inland the land rises steeply up to mountains over 1000 m high. The busy road outside the hotel goes west to the village along the coast – that's where we're eating tonight.
>
> See you soon, Jane x

Key words

Contour interval – the difference in height in metres shown by two contour lines next to each other

Contour lines – thin brown lines on maps that join together places at the same height above sea level

Relief – the height and shape of the land

Spot height – a black dot where the height of the land has been measured. Often on a hill top or along a road

Triangulation pillar – a concrete pillar once used in map-making, often on a hill top

Interpreting OS maps: relief and drainage

SKILLS 1

How to draw a cross-section

1 Use map **A**. Place the straight edge of a piece of paper along the section. Mark the start and end points on the paper (X and Y).
2 Mark the place where each contour line crosses. Note the heights of the contour lines.
3 Mark on major features, e.g. rivers, spot heights.
4 Draw a graph outline like that in **B**. A good guide for scale is 1 cm to 100 m for a 1:25 000 map.
5 Place your paper along the base of the graph. Put crosses on your graph at the correct heights and locations.
6 Draw a smooth freehand curve to join the crosses.
7 Add a title and labels for any key features, e.g. names of hills, rivers and roads.

For more help see page 122 of *SKILLS in geography*.

Key words

Cross-section – a diagram that shows the actual height and shape of the land, drawn as if the land has been cut in half

Drainage – the natural water features, e.g. rivers, lakes and marshes

Sketch map – a hand-drawn map, often a simpler version of another map

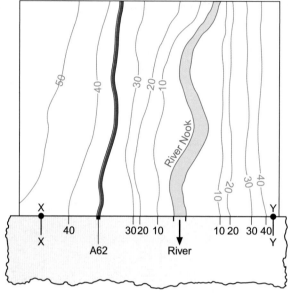

A How to draw a cross-section X to Y from an OS map

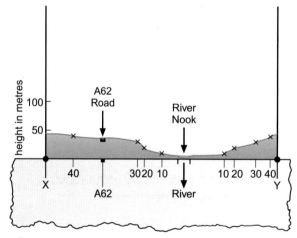

B How to draw a graph outline

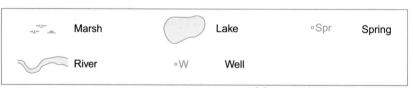

C Water features shown on OS maps

© Crown copyright, Licence no. 1000000230

RELIEF

Relief is the height and shape of the land. The contour lines, spot heights and triangulation pillars on an OS map can be used to find the relief of the land. This is very important, for example, if you are planning a walk. Will your route be flat, gently uphill or very steep? OS maps can also be used to draw a **cross-section** that shows what the landscape really looks like (see **A** and **B**).

DRAINAGE

The word '**drainage**' probably makes you think of drains and sewers, but in geography drainage means natural water features. On an OS map it is mainly the surface water features that are shown, such as rivers, lakes and marshes (**C**).

SKETCH MAPS

Sometimes an OS map looks very crowded and can be difficult to understand. You may only be interested in some features that are shown, such as the roads or a town or the physical features. Drawing a **sketch map** means that only the details you want need be shown. Sketch map **D** shows Cuckmere valley. It was drawn from the OS map on page 15.

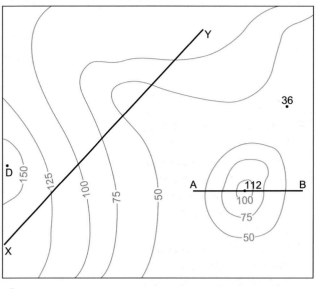

E Activity map, showing contour lines

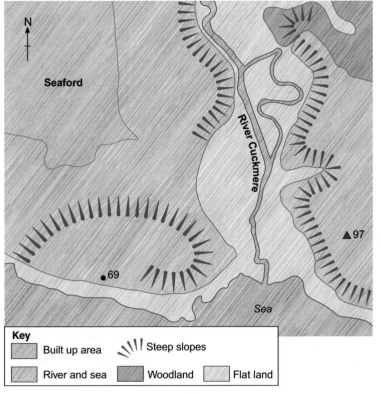

Key

- Built up area
- Steep slopes
- River and sea
- Woodland
- Flat land

 Sketch map of Cuckmere valley, scale 1:25 000

Activities

1. Draw cross-sections for lines A–B and X–Y from map **E**. Look at SKILLS 1 before you start.

2. Looking at map **E**, answer the following questions.
   a) About how high is point D?
   b) What kind of symbol shows the lowest land? How high is it?

3. Imagine you are walking from A to B on map **E**. Describe your route. Are you going uphill or downhill? Is it steep or gentle? What is the height of the land at each stage?

4. Choose a small area from the OS map of your local area, perhaps the area around your school. Using SKILLS 2, draw and label a simple sketch map to show the main features of the area. Use labels such as: *built-up area, housing, main road, woodland, farmland, river, flat land*.

SKILLS 2

How to draw a sketch map

1. Draw a frame for your sketch map – think about its size and shape.
2. In pencil, sketch the features you wish to show. Start with some accurate major features such as a coastline or road, or even lightly mark on the gridlines and numbers.
3. Colour in your sketch map. Add a key for the symbols and colours you have used.
4. Add a title, north sign and scale.

For more help see page 125 of *SKILLS in geography*.

Studying settlements on OS maps

>> **Understanding what a settlement hierarchy is**
>> **Learning about why people chose one site over another**

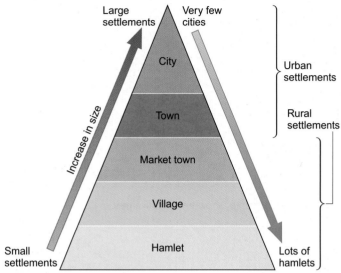

A A settlement hierarchy

A **settlement** is a place where people live. It can be anything from an isolated farm with one family to the very largest cities such as London and Birmingham. An OS map is a good starting point for looking at settlements. Look at **A**. When settlements are put into order of size or importance they form a **hierarchy**.

Settlements of different sizes have different types of shops and **services**. Think about a small village you know. It may have a Post Office, church and public house. But larger towns and cities have many more and larger services, such as secondary schools, hospitals and department stores (see **B**).

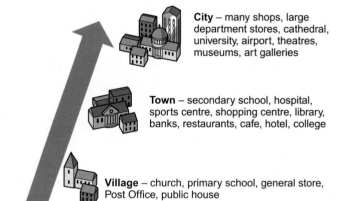

City – many shops, large department stores, cathedral, university, airport, theatres, museums, art galleries

Town – secondary school, hospital, sports centre, shopping centre, library, banks, restaurants, cafe, hotel, college

Village – church, primary school, general store, Post Office, public house

Hamlet – a post box

B A hierarchy based on services

SKILLS

Drawing a spider diagram

1 Use at least half a page and draw a circle (or box) in the centre.
2 Write the topic for your spider inside the circle.
3 Draw a line outwards from the circle for each bit of information you need to add.
4 Put your information into more circles at the end of each line.
5 Make your spider diagram attractive by colouring in the circles or adding small sketches.
6 Add a title.

Many settlements date back a long time and were very small to start with. People began to build settlements long before there were supermarkets for food, piped water and electricity, motor cars or bricks for building. People needed to support themselves from the local environment, so the **site** was very important. The site of a settlement is the physical land on which it is built. People looked for sites that had one or more natural advantages:

- a water supply from a river, lake or springs
- land not likely to be flooded
- flat land, easy to build on
- fertile soil to grow food, and grazing land for animals
- wood for fuel and building
- local stone and other resources for making buildings, pottery and weapons
- shelter from cold winds
- easy to defend from attackers
- easy crossing point of a river.

Look at map **C**. This shows the natural advantages or **siting factors** for Chester-le-Street in northeast England.

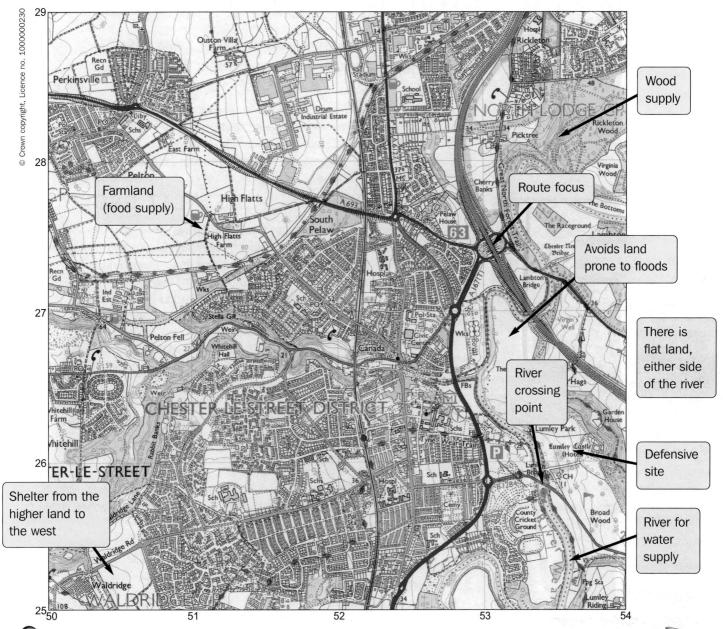

© Crown copyright. Licence no. 1000000230

Labels on the map:

- Wood supply
- Route focus
- Avoids land prone to floods
- There is flat land, either side of the river
- Defensive site
- River for water supply
- Farmland (food supply)
- River crossing point
- Shelter from the higher land to the west

C OS extract showing Chester-le-Street's natural advantages as a settlement site (scale 1:25 000)

Activities

(S)

1. Study a map of your local area. Choose *four or five* settlements of different sizes. Put them into a hierarchy like the one in **A**.

2. Choose *one* of the settlements from your hierarchy. Produce a spider diagram to show the different shops and services it has (see the SKILLS box on the opposite page).

3. You are the chief scribe for the first tribe to settle at Chester-le-Street. Write up your diary for the day the tribe chose to settle there. Say why you chose to settle at Chester-le-Street and draw a sketch map to go with your writing. (See page 125 of *SKILLS in geography* for more help on sketch maps.)

Key words

Hierarchy – settlements put into order of importance or size

Service – something that provides for people's needs, e.g. a shop, hairdresser, doctor, school

Settlement – a place where people live, e.g. farm, village, town, city

Site – the physical land on which a settlement is built

Siting factors – reasons for choosing a particular place for a settlement

Why do settlements grow?

>> **Learning about how and why settlements grow**
>> **Exploring how towns have different land-use zones**

As time went on, some early settlements grew into larger villages, then into towns and cities. This growth usually happened because the settlement was able to develop into a centre for trade or industry. This was usually because it was where roads and tracks met or was a river crossing point (a route focus).

WHY DID CHESTER-LE-STREET GROW?

Chester-le-Street grew into a market town in medieval times because it was sited at a bridging point across the River Wear. It was a meeting place of routes from north, south, east and west. People travelled from the surrounding area into Chester-le-Street to buy and sell goods. The market place is still very much in use on Fridays and Saturdays (**A**). Nearby Lumley Castle and Lambton Castle also both needed services that attracted workers to the settlement, for example, blacksmiths, bakers and carpenters.

Since that time industries and services have developed. The railway was built and eventually the A1(M). Today industries have come and gone, and Chester-le-Street is overshadowed by nearby Newcastle, Sunderland and Durham. It has grown, but largely as a commuter settlement. This means that people live in Chester-le-Street but travel to work in other areas.

As a settlement grows a pattern of land use is created that can be seen in many towns and cities (see **B**). **Land uses** are grouped together into *zones*. Map **C** shows how Chester-le-Street has grown and its different land-use zones. Table **D** shows some typical types of land use.

A The market in Chester-le-Street

Settlements tend to grow outwards from the centre – historic buildings such as churches and town halls are in the centre along with the market place, shops and offices. This area is called the Central Business District (**CBD**) today and it is often the focus of roads.

This is the zone around the CBD. During the Industrial Revolution railways were built and factories and workshops developed. Housing was needed for the workers so rows of terraced houses were built close to the workplace. Can you think why?

As the settlement continued to grow, housing estates were built beyond the terraces where land was cheaper and there was more space. Today new housing estates continue to develop and new industrial estates, business parks and shopping centres have been built on the edges of the town.

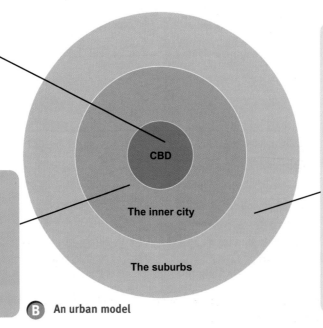

CBD

The inner city

The suburbs

B An urban model

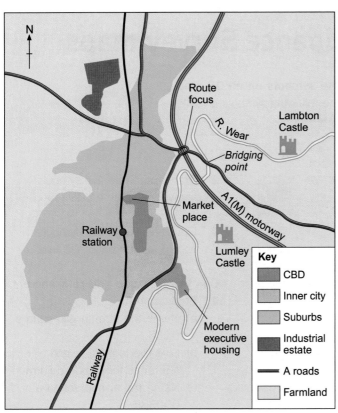

Key

▨ CBD	
▨ Inner city	
▨ Suburbs	
▨ Industrial estate	
— A roads	
▨ Farmland	

C The growth of Chester-le-Street

Land-use zone	Examples
Residential	Different types of housing, e.g. grid layout of terraced rows, winding avenues of more modern suburbs and housing estates
Industrial	Works, factories
Commercial	Shops, offices
Agricultural	Farmland, market gardens
Educational	Schools, universities
Religious	Churches, temples, mosques
Communications	Roads, railways, canals
Historical / tourist	Campsites, museums, information centres, castles

D Land-use types

a

b

c

d

E Chester-le-Street

Activities

1 Study the list below. Using table **D**, decide what type of land use each one belongs to.

> motorway   Town Hall   bungalow   hairdresser's   college

2 Use a map of your local area. Give the four-figure grid references to identify the three different landuse zones given in **B**. (See SKILLS, pages 18–19 for more help.)

3 Study the photographs of Chester-le Street (**E**). For each photograph, say which landuse zone in **B** it belongs to, and give a reason why.

4 a) In pairs, study the model in **B** and the sketch map **C** of Chester-le-Street. In what ways does the sketch map not fit the model? Can you think of reasons why?

b) Form groups to discuss your ideas. Ask someone from each group to present the group's ideas to the class.

Key words

Central Business District – zone of shops, offices and historic buildings, often in the centre of a town

Inner City – zone of industries and terraces built in the nineteenth century

Land use – what the land is used for, usually in zones

Suburbs – zone of housing estates built since 1920 on the outskirts of towns

Urban – the larger settlements of towns and cities

Using Ordnance Survey maps

Do you understand the symbols on an OS map?

1 What do each of the following symbols mean?

a) ✗ 1066   b) ══════   c) ▲   d) CH   PC   PO   TH

A OS map extract of Salisbury, scale 1:25 000

© Crown copyright, Licence no. 100000230

2 Draw and name *five* symbols shown in red on an OS map.

3 Draw and name *five* symbols shown in blue on an OS map.

Can you now use grid references?

4 Study map **A**.
a) Name the farm in grid square 0136.
b) Give the four-figure grid reference for Deptford Farm.
c) Name the symbol found at 000386.
d) Give the six-figure grid reference of the public telephone in Wylye.

Do you understand distance, direction and height?

5 Study map **A**.
a) In which direction are you travelling if you drive along the secondary road from near Bilbury Farm into Wylye?
b) Measure the distance along the A303T shown on the map extract.
c) At what height is the hill at grid reference 025366?

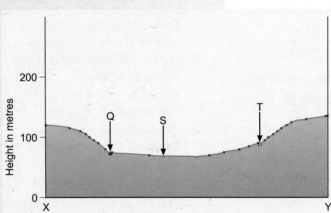

B Cross-section from X to Y on map A

Can you use an OS map to find out about relief and drainage?

6 **B** shows a cross-section from X to Y on map **A**.
a) Features Q, S and T are a road, a river and a railway line. Which is which?
b) What is the height of the land at Y?

7 Describe the relief of the land shown on the cross-section.

8 Draw a sketch map of **A** to show the main features of the relief and drainage.

9 Give reasons why there is very little settlement in grid squares 0236 and 0137.

Investigating your local area

Do you know what this type of housing is called? Is it old or new?
Are there houses like these near to where you live?

Learning objectives

What are you going to learn about in this chapter?

> The types of housing in the UK and in your home area
> How to plan and undertake an investigation of housing in your local area
> Other methods of local investigation using secondary data
> How to use questionnaires in geographical investigations

 **Housing in Durham**

What is the housing like in your home area?

>> **Investigating types of housing in the UK**
>> **Drawing bar graphs**

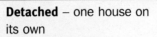

Key words

Detached – one house on its own
Flat – a one-level living area
Semi-detached – two houses joined together
Terraced – houses joined together in a line

What do you know about the geography of the area where you live? One of the main aims of this chapter is to encourage you to observe your local area more closely, and through geographical eyes. Remember what you read on page 6: 'To be a good geographer, you need to be good at observing ...'.

An obvious starting point for a local study is an investigation of houses. Everyone in the UK needs shelter, because the weather is cool, wet and windy for much of the year. How many hours do you spend indoors on winter weekends?

What type of house do you live in? Can you describe it fully?

The house in photograph **A** is over 50 years old. Look carefully at its features. In what ways is it different from **semi-detached** houses built on modern housing estates?

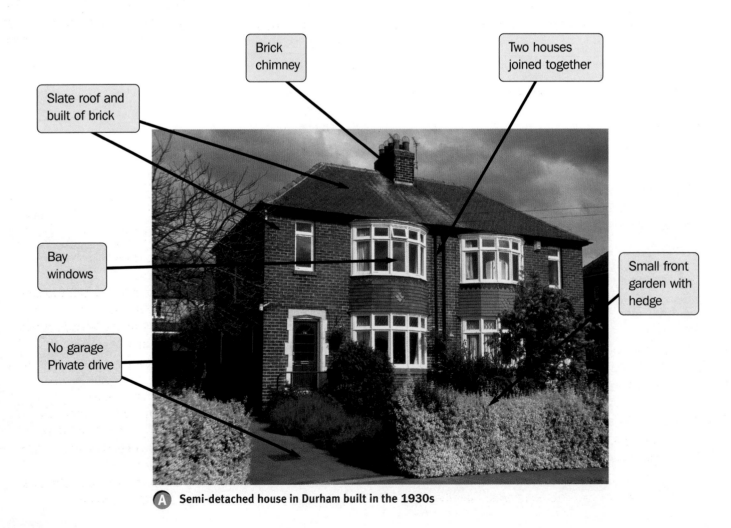

Brick chimney

Two houses joined together

Slate roof and built of brick

Bay windows

Small front garden with hedge

No garage Private drive

A Semi-detached house in Durham built in the 1930s

THE MAIN TYPES OF HOUSING IN THE UK

B This row of terraced houses was built over 100 years ago

C A detached house built in the 1990s – notice the double garage

D A tower block of flats in Birmingham – how many storeys can you see?

1 Terraced houses

Terraced houses are built in a line, all joined together, like the ones in photograph **B**. They were built in large numbers in the UK from Victorian times, in the nineteenth century, until about 1930. Many of them were built to house people working in nearby factories.

2 Semi-detached houses

A **semi-detached** house is joined to another house on only one side, as in photograph **A**. They were first built in large numbers in the UK in the 1930s. 'Semis' are the most common type of house on many housing estates built since 1960.

3 Detached houses

A **detached** house stands alone with space all around it (photograph **C**). The percentage of detached houses on new housing estates has increased since 1960. This is because more people can afford these houses, which cost more because they use more land.

4 Flats

In **flats**, as in bungalows, people live on one level. Other types of houses have stairs leading to different levels. By building high, more people can live on less land (photograph **D**). Many tower blocks were built in the 1960s in inner city areas.

Activities

1 a) Name the type of housing you live in.

   b) Draw a sketch, or use a photograph, of the front of your house. Add labels to describe its features (look back at photograph **A**).

2 Choose *one* type of house different from yours from photographs **B–D**. Sketch or trace it and label its main features. (See page 125 of *SKILLS in geography* for help.)

3 a) Carry out a survey of where people in your class live to find out what type of housing is the most common. Once you have collected the information, add up the totals for each type. Then draw a vertical bar graph to show the results (see the SKILLS box for how to do this).

   b) Looking at the results, can you think of any reasons why one type of housing is more common than the others?

SKILLS

How to draw a vertical bar graph

1 Make a frame with two lines (called *axes*).
2 Label what each axis shows.
3 On the *vertical* axis (up the side) make a scale, large enough for the highest number.
4 From the *horizontal axis* (along the bottom) draw bars of equal width.

For more help see page 123 of *SKILLS in geography*.

How to plan an investigation of housing

>> **Learning about investigations**
>> **Finding out how to carry out a survey**

There are four stages in a geographical enquiry that make up an investigation. Look at **A**. You are going to see how these four stages can be used in a geographical investigation of housing.

STAGE 1: PLANNING

Careful planning is important. Let us assume that your group has met and agreed this title:

What are the differences in housing between areas A and B?

What needs to be done next?

1 Choose areas A and B.

Area A could be near to your school and B where you live, or A and B could be two areas where different members of the class live. If you live in a rural area, A and B could be in two different villages.

2 Think about the information to be collected.

In this example, the group has decided to do a survey of housing and **environmental quality**.

3 What should be included in this kind of survey?

After much discussion the group decided that they would observe four factors:

- *Housing layout and design*. Are the houses attractive and well spaced? Or is the housing not very interesting, with the houses packed together?

- *Gardens and greenery*. Are there gardens or grass and trees to improve the area's appearance? Or is there little or no greenery?

- *Car parking*. Are there garages and places for cars to park off the road? Or must cars be parked on the road?

- *Overall appearance*. Does it look good, tidy and clean? Or does it look run down, with signs of damage and graffiti?

4 Make a recording sheet for the marks for each house like the one in **B**.

5 Decide on the number of houses to be surveyed and which ones to include. A similar number should be surveyed in area A and area B.

It is a good idea to work in pairs when giving marks for environmental quality. Each person suggests a score. If you do not agree, use the average score.

Planning
This is thinking about what to do and asking yourself questions.
- What do I want to find out?
- Where am I going to do the investigation?

Collecting information
This is mainly done by **fieldwork**. Fieldwork can be done by:
- observing
- measuring
- counting.

Presenting the information collected
This is done by showing the information:
- in tables and graphs
- using labelled sketches and photographs
- on maps.

Writing about what the information shows
- Describe what the tables, graphs, etc. show.
- Look for any similarities and differences.
- Is there a pattern?

A The four stages of an enquiry

Name of house / housing area								
Factors	**Good**	**5**	**4**	**3**	**2**	**1**	**0**	**Bad**
Housing layout and design	Attractive and well spaced							Unattractive and closely packed
Gardens and greenery	Good-looking							No greenery
Car parking	Garages and parking spaces							On-road parking only
Overall appearance	Good and clean							Run down and damaged

B Recording sheet for a housing and environmental quality survey

Activities

1   Look back at the houses and housing areas in photographs **A–D** on pages 32 and 33. For each photograph, you are going to give a score out of 5 for the factors on recording sheet **B**.

a) Make a recording sheet like the one below. (You could use a spreadsheet package to produce it on a computer.)

Recording sheet of marks awarded					
Houses	**Housing layout and design**	**Gardens and greenery**	**Car parking**	**Overall appearance**	**Total marks**
A	5 4 3 2 1 0	5 4 3 2 1 0	5 4 3 2 1 0	5 4 3 2 1 0	
B	5 4 3 2 1 0	5 4 3 2 1 0	5 4 3 2 1 0	5 4 3 2 1 0	
C	5 4 3 2 1 0	5 4 3 2 1 0	5 4 3 2 1 0	5 4 3 2 1 0	
D	5 4 3 2 1 0	5 4 3 2 1 0	5 4 3 2 1 0	5 4 3 2 1 0	

b) Working by yourself, look carefully at photographs **A–D** on pages 32 and 33. Give a mark out of 5 for each factor. Fill in the recording sheet by putting circles around the marks awarded.

2   When you have finished, compare your marks with those of at least two other people around you. Have you been more or less generous than them? Do you want to change any of your marks?

3   a) When you are happy with your marks, add up the total marks for each house.

b) Which house got most marks? Explain why it has done so well.

c) Which one got least marks? Explain why it has done badly.

4   a) Think of *one* other factor that could have been used in a housing survey like this.

b) Would it have changed the order you put the houses in? Explain your answer.

Key word

Environmental quality – how good or bad a human landscape looks

Carrying out an investigation of housing

>> Practising your investigation skills
>> Collecting, recording and presenting information

EXAMPLES OF HOUSES AND HOUSING AREAS

Housing area A

Housing area B

STAGE 2: COLLECTING INFORMATION

When the planning is complete, it is time for **fieldwork**. Observe the houses and housing areas and give them marks. Note the marks down on a recording sheet.

Look at the four photographs of the houses and housing areas on the opposite page. All were taken in the same city. As an example of what to do, look at how the marks have been awarded on the recording sheet below.

Recording sheet of marks awarded					
Houses	Housing layout and design	Gardens and greenery	Car parking	Overall appearance	Total marks
A1	5 4 3 2 ①0	5 4 3 2 ①0	5 4 3 2 1 ⓪	5 4 ③2 1 0	
A2	5 4 3 ②1 0	5 4 3 2 1 ⓪	5 4 3 2 1 ⓪	5 4 3 ②1 0	
B1	5 ④3 2 1 0	5 4 ③2 1 0	5 ④3 2 1 0	5 ④3 2 1 0	
B2	⑤4 3 2 1 0	⑤4 3 2 1 0	⑤4 3 2 1 0	⑤4 3 2 1 0	

STAGE 3: PRESENTING THE INFORMATION COLLECTED

One way to show the results is on bar graphs. It is best to keep the same scale for both graphs so that the results can be compared. This makes it easier to pick out similarities and differences.

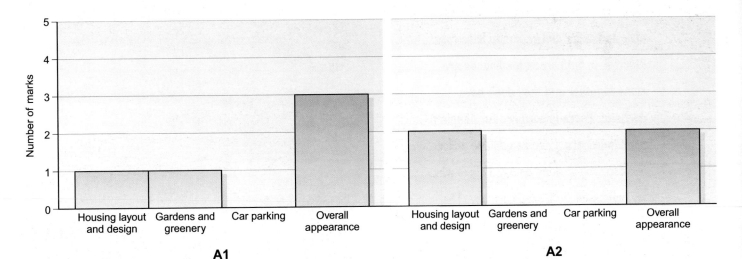

A1   **A2**

C **Results of housing and environmental quality investigation in area A**

Activities

1. a) Add up the total marks for each housing area.
   b) Work out the average mark for each one (total divided by 4).
   c) Rank them in order from highest to lowest.
2. Draw bar graphs to show the results for B1 and B2. (You can either draw them by hand or use a computer graph package.) See page 123 for more help.

Key word

Fieldwork – work done in the area under study, out of the classroom and often out-of-doors

Writing up the housing investigation

>> Understanding *what* to include in your report
>> Writing up a fieldwork investigation

STAGE 4: WRITING ABOUT WHAT THE INFORMATION SHOWS

Writing up is often the most difficult part. One way of writing up this investigation on housing might be:

- First, write about what is shown by the photographs, record sheet, average marks and bar graph for area A (see location map **B** below).
- Next, do the same for area B.
- Then, describe the similarities and differences between housing areas A and B.
- Next, try to explain them.
- Finally, write a short conclusion.

You can see what a student has written up about area A in **A**.

The photographs show two areas of terraced houses. The houses in A1 are small and have only two storeys, whereas those in A2 are bigger. One house has an attic and cellar and seems to have four storeys. In both areas the houses are close together and they don't have gardens. There is nowhere for people to park their cars. I can see double yellow lines to stop parking on A2. This is why my marks for both areas are low. The highest bar is for appearance in A1. I think A1 looks better than A2 because of the flowerpots and fresh paint around the windows. The average mark for A1 is a bit higher because of this.

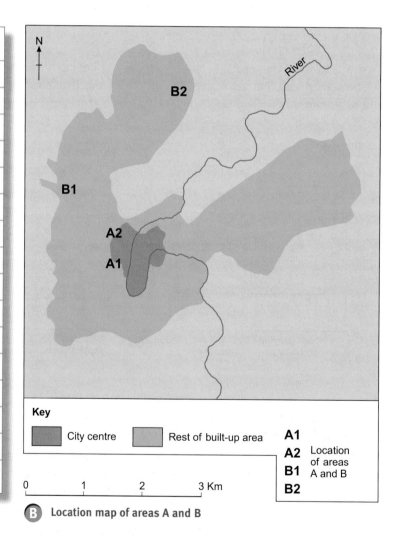

Key

■ City centre   ■ Rest of built-up area

A1
A2 Location of areas A and B
B1
B2

0   1   2   3 Km

(A) A Year 7 student's writing up about area A

(B) Location map of areas A and B

A1

A2

At the top right is a diagram of concentric circles labelled:

CBD · The inner city · The suburbs

C Land-use zones

Where are the areas located?

Map **B** shows locations for housing areas A and B. Area A is near to the city centre; it is located in the older part of the city. Area B is near to the edge of the built-up area, in the newer part. Knowing locations makes it easier to explain the differences between these two housing areas. The locations of these houses fit the expected pattern of land uses found in most UK towns and cities (diagram **C**). Land-use zones are laid out in circles around the CBD (see page 28).

Activities

(S)

1 Write about area B. Use the example **A** as a guide.

2 a) Make and fill in a summary chart for similarities and differences like the one below. Use the marks you gave in Stage 2.

   b) After calculating the average marks (from page 37), write a comment to explain why the marks are high, low or in the middle.

B1

B2

SIMILARITIES AND DIFFERENCES				
	Area A (older part)		Area B (newer part)	
	A1	A2	B1	B2
Types of houses				
Housing layout and design				
Gardens and greenery				
Car parking				
Overall appearance				
Average marks				
Comment				

3 Write a short paragraph about differences in housing and environmental quality between the older and newer parts of the city. This will be your conclusion.

4 a) Now you can carry out your own fieldwork investigation of housing in your local area, using the work you have just completed as a guide. Remember to follow the four stages of an enquiry.

   b) Present your results using tables, labelled photographs and graphs. (For more help see pages 121–125 of SKILLS in geography.)

SKILLS

How to write up a fieldwork investigation

1 Write about what your tables, graphs, diagrams and maps show.

2 Mention any similarities and differences.

3 Explain the patterns shown.

4 Write a conclusion, bearing in mind what you were trying to investigate.

Other methods of investigation in geography

>> **Knowing how to find and use secondary data**
>> **Introducing the census as a data source**

Key words

Census – information collected by the government about people, such as how many people and where they live
Neighbourhood – a small district in a town or city
Primary data – information collected by fieldwork
Secondary data – information collected by someone else before you use it

Most people enjoy doing fieldwork, and it is a good way to collect information. However, you can still investigate in geography without going out of school.

Information that you collect by fieldwork is called **primary data**, because you are the *first* person to collect this information. When working from books or the Internet, you will be using **secondary data**. Someone else has collected the information, so that you are at least the *second* person who has used it.

There are many sources of secondary data. For example, you can find out about:

- **the weather** – from newspapers and satellite images
- **tourism** – from local and national tourist offices and from travel brochures
- **population** – from the **census**
- **housing** – from estate agents and property advertisements in newspapers.

Estate agents' windows have useful information about house types and prices in the local area (photograph **A**). Most estate agents have their own websites as well.

Obtaining secondary information has never been easier, thanks to the Internet. In fact, the main problem today is information overload – too much information. It is difficult to search through all the information on websites to find the information you need.

USING THE CENSUS WEBSITE FOR LOCAL STUDY

The results of the 2001 census in the UK are now online at the Government Statistics website.

Each small area in the UK is called a **neighbourhood** in the census. The most useful data for studies of your local area are the *neighbourhood statistics*. The census gives useful geographical statistics about, for example, population, health, employment, housing and households.

To find your own neighbourhood statistics, follow these steps:

1 Go to www.heinemann.co.uk/hotlinks and enter the Express code **6437P**. Click on the link for Chapter 3, pages 40 and 41.
2 A little way down the webpage look for: **Local Authority profiles**. Click on the first letter of the name of your Local Authority.
3 Find your Local Authority and click on **Profile**.
4 Look for and click on to **Neighbourhood Statistics**.
5 You will see a page like web page **B**. Enter your home or school postcode in the box.
6 For housing information, scroll down to **Housing and Households**.

A Estate agents are a useful source of information about housing

Neighbourhood Statistics

Welcome to Neighbourhood Statistics

Use this site to view, compare or download statistics for local areas on a wide range of subjects including population, crime, health and housing.

Please choose one of the options below:

Summary statistics for your area
Please enter your full postcode or a city or town name (England and Wales only)

[   ] **GO**

B A page from the census website

People living in different types of housing (%)	Birmingham (**D**, page 33)	Durham (**A**, page 32)
Detached	11	19
Semi-detached	35	49
Terraced	31	25
Flats	23	7
Total population	977 000	88 000

C Examples of UK census data (2001)

Activities

S

1 a) Using table **C**, list from highest to lowest percentage the different types of housing in Birmingham and Durham.

  b) Which type of housing shows the greatest difference in percentage between the two cities? Don't forget to show your working.

  c) Can you suggest a reason for this large difference?

2 a) Go to the census website at www.heinemann.co.uk/hotlinks (enter express code **6437P**) and, download data for **Housing and Households** for your neighbourhood.

  b) Note the percentages for the four different types of housing and then draw a bar graph to show these percentages.

  c) How different are they from those for Birmingham? Answer as fully as you can.

3 Now you are ready to prepare a report on your local area. You can *either* prepare an ICT presentation *or* make a display on a sheet of A4 paper. Use the title '**Types of housing and house prices in _____**' (*insert the name of your local area*). Remember to use primary and secondary sources and illustrate your report with labelled pictures, sketches and graphs.

4 Look at the average house prices for 2001 in the Table below.

	Durham	**England and Wales**
Detached	£112 000	£180 000
Semi-detached	£61 000	£101 000
Terraced	£57 000	£90 000
All types of housing	£71 000	£120 000

  a) Draw bar graphs to show the data for house prices. (See pages 122 and 123 of *SKILLS in geography*.)

  b) Describe what the graphs show about house prices in Durham compared with the rest of the country.

  c) Why are average house prices called '*secondary data*'?

Using questionnaires

>> **Creating a good questionnaire**
>> **Drawing pictographs**

Asking people questions is another good method of investigation in geography. A questionnaire is a set of questions that you ask people to answer. Questionnaires are useful for finding out what people do or think.

Using questionnaires is the best way to discover where people:

- do their shopping
- travel to work
- go on holiday.

It is the only way that you can find out what people think about any changes being planned. People can be asked to give their views about plans for building a new supermarket, or plans to make a street traffic-free. The questionnaire on the opposite page was designed to find out how people spend their holidays.

How many people in photograph **A** are shoppers? What are they planning to buy? Are they locals or first-time visitors? Only by using questionnaires can you find out answers to questions like these.

Thinking up good questions for a questionnaire needs skill and care. You must not ask questions that can cause offence, like the students in **B**. Without the help of other people no useful information can be collected.

A People in Birmingham city centre

SKILLS

How to draw a pictograph

1 Choose a symbol that looks like what you are trying to show (e.g. £ for money).
2 If total numbers are small, use one symbol per person or item.
3 If total numbers are large, use one symbol to represent 10, 100 or more.
4 Try to make each symbol the same size.

For more help see page 122 of *SKILLS in geography*.

B How to upset people

1   Use the questionnaire below to find out how the people in your class spent their holidays.

   a) Working alone, fill in a copy of the questionnaire below.

   b) As a class, put the answers together in a summary. *Either* write them down *or* enter them on a data base already set up on the computer.

2   Work in a small group or by yourself.

   a) Find out how many people stayed in the United Kingdom. What percentage of your class was this?

   b) Now draw a pictograph to show the numbers who:

   • stayed in the UK

   • went abroad.

   (See the SKILLS box, page 42, for more help.)

3   Now use an outline map of the world, with the UK clearly shown.

   a) Mark and name the place where you live.

   b) Mark and name each place visited.

   c) Draw a straight line from your home area to the place visited for each person.

4   Look at the results for your class for Activity 3. Are they what you expected? Are there any surprises? Answer as fully as you can.

Holiday survey questionnaire

Your main holiday this year

Please answer these questions for your main holiday this year.
The main holiday is the longest one you had away from home.
If you did not have a holiday away from home this year, answer for the best day visit you had.

1   **Name the main place you stayed in or visited.**

   Place _____   Country _____

2   **How did you travel there?** Tick one box for the main method of travel.

   Car ☐   Train ☐   Ship ☐   Air ☐   Bus / coach ☐   Other ☐ : state the method _____

3   **For how long did you go?** Tick one box.

   1 day ☐   2–6 days ☐   7–10 days ☐   11–15 days ☐   Longer ☐ : state how long _____

4   **What type of accommodation did you use?** Tick one box.

   Hotel ☐   Apartment / villa ☐   Camping / caravan ☐   None ☐   Other ☐ : state type _____

5   **What did you do on the holiday or visit?** Tick all the boxes that apply.

Spent time on the beach	☐	Sightseeing in cities	☐
Swam in the sea	☐	Sightseeing outside cities	☐
Played sport	☐	Watched sport	☐
Hiking / walking	☐	Shopping	☐
Visited theme parks / amusements	☐	Visited museums / art galleries	☐
Went to discos / cinemas	☐	Went to concerts / theatres	☐

Investigating your local area

Do you now know how to set up a geographical investigation using primary data?

1 An investigation into shopping using a questionnaire is being set up. Look at the questionnaire below.
   a) Copy and complete questions 3 and 4.
   b) Think of another question that you could write out for question 5. (Hint – look back at the holiday questionnaire.)

Shopping investigation questionnaire

We are investigating shopping habits in this area. Please answer the questions below.

1 Name the place where most of your weekly shopping is done.
   Place _____

2 How do you usually travel there? Tick one box.
   Walk ☐   Car ☐   Bus ☐   Train ☐   Other ☐ : state the method _____

3 How long does it take you to get there?

4 How often do you go there to shop?

5 (Add your own question here.) _____

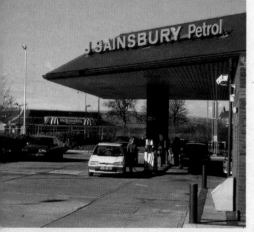

Ⓐ **Many garages have shops used by non-motorists**

Some questions used by students on questionnaires are not useful. Can you improve them?

2 Choose *three* of the questions below. Write down why each one is a bad question.

Question letter	Why it is a bad question
1 _____	_____
2 _____	_____
3 _____	_____

A Do you come here often?
B Are you male or female?
C How much money have you got to spend today?
D Do you like shopping here? Yes or no?
E How many marks out of 10 would you give this shopping centre?

---

3 Now choose *one* of the questions and try to make it better.

» 4   What is the UK?

The Houses of Parliament stand next to the River Thames in London, the centre of government for the UK. Can you name the four countries that make up the UK? What do people call the clock in the photograph?

Learning objectives

What are you going to learn about in this chapter?

> The countries that make up the UK

> The physical geography of the UK

> How the UK can be divided up

> Whether there is a North–South divide

> How London is different

> What football can teach us about geography

(A) Westminster and the River Thames, in London

How is the UK made up?

>> **Understanding how the UK is made up**
>> **Drawing a divided bar graph**

The British Isles are made up of two big **islands** and many small ones. Two countries occupy them – the United Kingdom (UK) and the Republic of Ireland (map **A**). Although the greatest concentration of islands is off the west coast of Scotland, islands are everywhere. In the far north are the Shetland Islands; in the far south, off the coast of France, are the Channel Islands.

Four countries were united together to form the United Kingdom of Great Britain and Northern Ireland (map **C**). Scotland was united to England and Wales in 1706 and Ireland in 1801. The southern counties of Ireland left the union in 1922 to form the Republic of Ireland. Although people in Scotland, Wales and Northern Ireland have control of some of their own affairs, the big decisions are still taken by Parliament in London, the **capital city** of the UK.

There are many differences in the history and traditions of the four countries. Ancient languages, such as Welsh and Gaelic, are still spoken in areas of Wales, Scotland and Ireland. Welsh people are noted for their love of music. Scotland is known for its wild scenery, its whisky, haggis, kilts and, of course, the Loch Ness monster.

Although they share a common flag, the Union Jack, each country has its own flag (see **B**). Can you see how the Union Jack was formed by using the crosses of St George, St Andrew and St Patrick? Thousands of people wave these flags at international football matches (**D**).

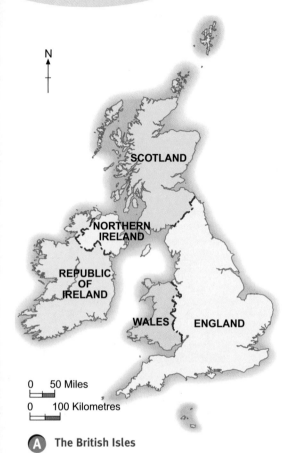

A The British Isles

Key words

Capital city – the centre of government in a country
Island – area of land surrounded by water

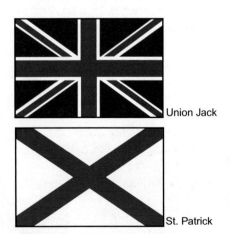

Union Jack

St. Patrick

B Flags of the United Kingdom

St. Andrew

St. George

C The United Kingdom

D Football supporters often paint their faces

	Area (km²)	%	Population (millions)	%
England	130 000	53	49.2	83
Northern Ireland	14 000	6	1.7	3
Scotland	77 000	32	5.1	9
Wales	21 000	9	2.9	5

F Information about the UK (2001)

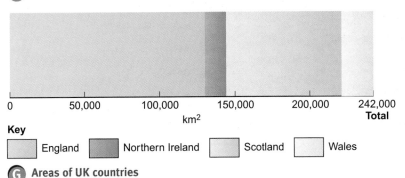

```
0      50,000   100,000   150,000   200,000   242,000
                    km²                          Total
```

Key

| | England | | Northern Ireland | | Scotland | | Wales |

G Areas of UK countries

```
0      50 Miles
0      100 Kilometres
```

E Great Britain

Activities

1 a) Study map **E** and name the countries that make up Great Britain.

   b) On the front of a passport is written: UNITED KINGDOM OF GREAT BRITAIN AND NORTHERN IRELAND. Why is United Kingdom the correct name for the country, not Great Britain?

2 a) Look at table **F**. What was the total population of the UK in 2001?

   b) Now look at graph **G**. Draw a divided bar graph to show population percentages for the four countries (see the SKILLS box). Add a key.

3 Population density is the number of people per square kilometre. To work out the population density of England, divide the number of people by the area of the country:

     49 200 000 ÷ 130 000 = 378.5
     population ÷ area = *population density*

   Now work out the population densities for the other three countries in the UK.

4 People living in Wales, Scotland and Northern Ireland often complain that England dominates the UK too much. Do the figures for area and population in **F** help to explain why England seems to dominate? Answer as fully as you can.

SKILLS

How to draw a divided bar graph

Look at graph **G** for a finished example.

1 Add up the values and make a total.

2 Draw a bar for the total value.

3 The bar can be either vertical or horizontal.

4 Add the scale to the sides of the bar.

5 Plot the different values.

For more help, see page 122 of *SKILLS in geography*

The physical geography of the UK

>> Finding out the UK's main physical features

>> Understanding how colours are used in maps

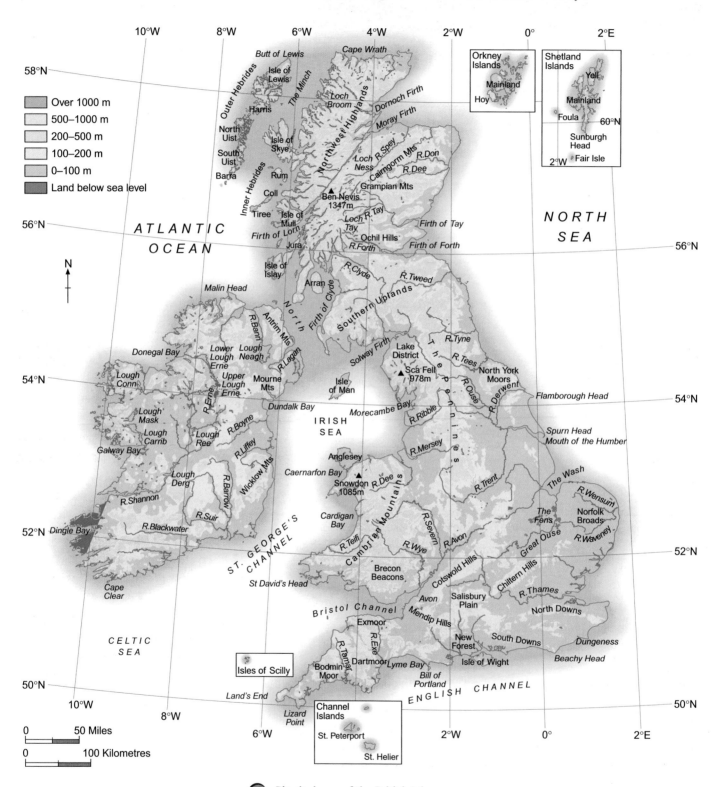

Legend:
- Over 1000 m
- 500–1000 m
- 200–500 m
- 100–200 m
- 0–100 m
- Land below sea level

(A) Physical map of the British Isles

Do you remember what physical geography is? If not, look back at Chapters 1 and 2. A physical geographer is most interested in the UK's **relief** and **drainage**.

Look at map **A**. Maps like these can give you lots of information about relief and drainage. For example, you can find the longest rivers. At 322 km (200 miles) long the River Severn is the UK's longest river; the River Thames comes a close second. How do the UK's rivers compare in size with the world's longest rivers? Look back to page 13 in Chapter 1.

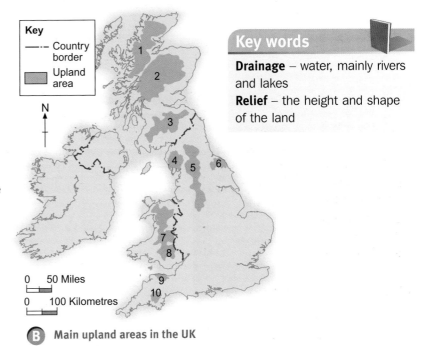

Key

——·— Country border

▨ Upland area

N

0   50 Miles

0   100 Kilometres

B Main upland areas in the UK

Key words

Drainage – water, mainly rivers and lakes
Relief – the height and shape of the land

Activities

1 a) Make a table like the one below. Give it the title: 'The highest mountains in Great Britain'. Fill it in using map **A** and an atlas.

Country	Highest mountain	Height (metres)	Upland area around it
England			
Scotland			
Wales			

b) Make another table and give it the title: 'The longest rivers in England'. Fill it in using map **A** and an atlas.

River	Source (where river starts from)	Mouth (where river reaches the sea)
Severn		
Tees		
Trent		
Thames		

2 The main upland areas in the UK are numbered 1 to 10 on map **B**. Use an atlas to find their names (see SKILLS, page 00, for more help).

3 Find the *Fens* on map **A**. In what way are the Fens different from the rest of the country?

4 The physical features of the *west coast* of Great Britain are different from those of the *east coast*. From map **A**, can you name *two* differences?

5 a) On map **A**, which colour is used to show lowland areas less than 100 m above sea level?

b) Why do you think this colour is used for showing lowlands?

c) Where in Britain are the largest lowland areas found?

6 a) On map **A**, which colours are used to show upland areas (above 200m)?

b) Why do you think these colours are used?

c) Where in Britain are most upland areas located?

Dividing up the UK

>> **Understanding the different physical areas of the UK**
>> **Learning how the government divides up the UK into regions**

How can the UK be divided up to make it easier to study? There are many different ways. For example, in physical geography Great Britain can be split into two parts – Highland Britain and Lowland Britain (map **A**). In human geography there can be even more divisions. For example, the UK government splits the UK into twelve regions. These regions and their counties are used by human geographers to study housing or population density.

HIGHLAND AND LOWLAND BRITAIN

B *The Giant's Causeway.* Can you see all the vertical lines of weakness in the rock? Despite these, basalt is a hard rock. It resists the battering of the waves for a long time.

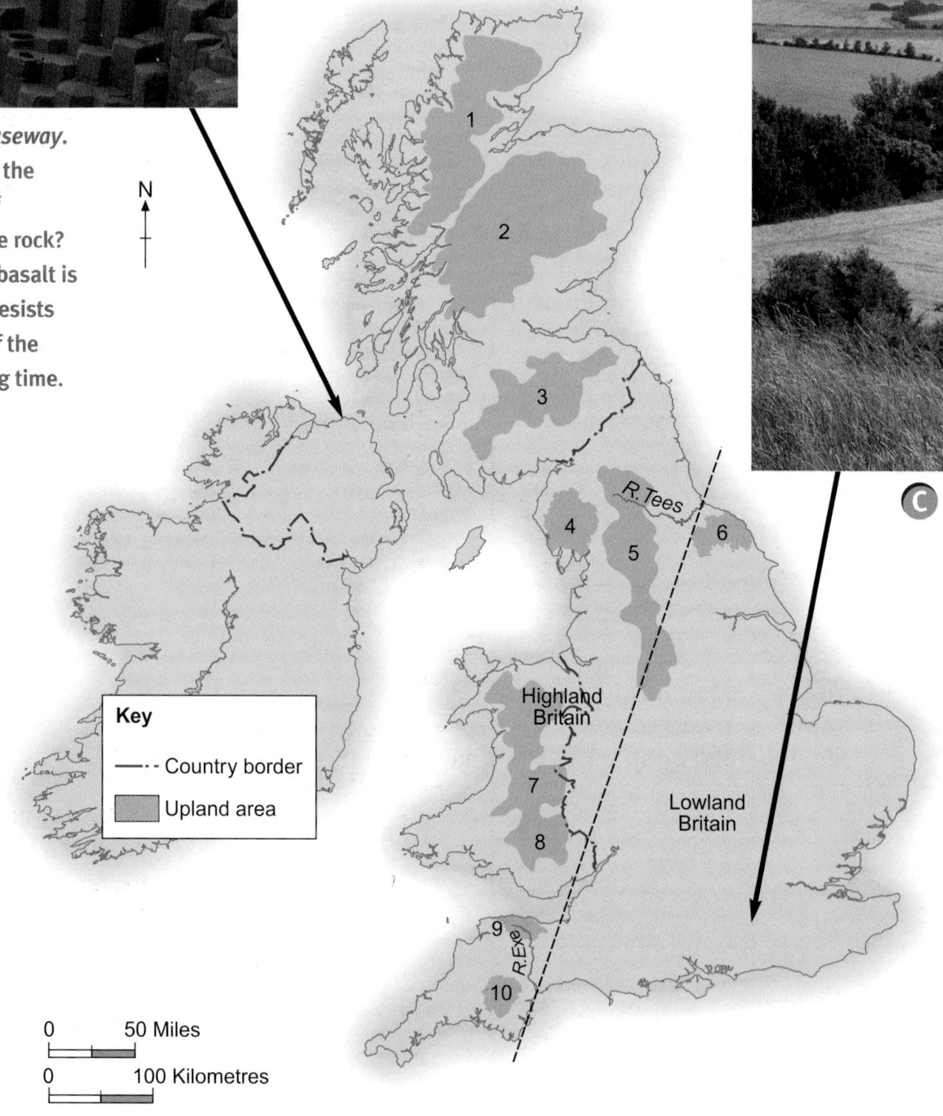

C *The Vale of Sussex.* This lowland is made of clay. It is drained by the River Ouse. There are two other big rivers in England called Ouse. Where do they flow?

N

R. Tees

Highland Britain

Lowland Britain

R. Exe

Key

-- · -- Country border

Upland area

0   50 Miles

0   100 Kilometres

A Highland Britain and Lowland Britain

A straight line can be drawn across England from north east to south west (see map **A**). This line runs from the mouth of the River Tees to the mouth of the River Exe. Highland Britain is the land north and west of the line. Lowland Britain is to the south and east, where most land is below 200 metres above sea level. Now look back at map **A** on page 48. Do you think it is a successful way of splitting the UK into two physical regions?

Geologists can explain this division for us. Rocks in the north and west of the UK are old and hard. Examples are granite and basalt. **Erosion** is slow because of rock hardness. On the other hand, most rocks in the south and east were formed more recently and are softer. Examples are clays and sands, which are eroded easily and quickly.

HOW THE GOVERNMENT DIVIDES UP THE UK

The UK government divides the country up into twelve administrative regions (map **D**) for statistical purposes. There are nine regions in England, plus Scotland, Wales and Northern Ireland. One important city from each region (outside London) is named on the map. These cities are **regional centres**. Many people from surrounding areas go there to work and shop.

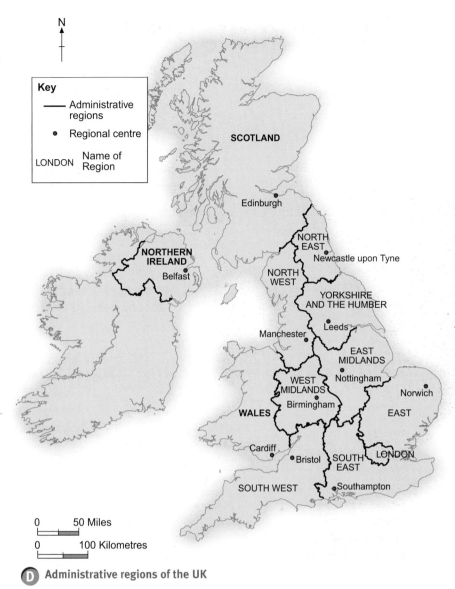

Key
—— Administrative regions
• Regional centre
LONDON Name of Region

 Administrative regions of the UK

Activities

1. Draw or trace a sketch map of Great Britain to show the division into Highland and Lowland Britain using **A**.

2. Make a table to show differences between Highland Britain and Lowland Britain (see also map **A**, page 48). Use the headings in the table below.

	Highland Britain	**Lowland Britain**
Height of the land		
Types of rock		
Named examples of areas		

3. a) Using map **D** name the administrative region you live in.
   b) Which is your nearest regional centre?
   c) For what reasons do you and your family go there?

Key words

Erosion – wearing away of the Earth's surface by rivers, waves and ice
Geologist – person who studies the Earth's crust and its rocks
Regional centre – a large city, with many shops and offices, that serves the area around it

North and South

>> **Becoming aware of the North–South divide**
>> **Using mental maps and sketches**

Have you heard of the North–South divide within England? It refers to the gap between the poor North and the rich South. This division of the country into two regions is based on **economic** factors, because it is based on wealth.

THE NORTH

Where does the North begin? Not everyone agrees about this. However, a curved line drawn from the southern side of the Humber **estuary** to the southern side of the Mersey estuary is a good starting point. This line runs south of Hull, Sheffield, Manchester and Liverpool. Everyone agrees that these four cities, which grew fast and were prosperous during the **Industrial Revolution**, are located in the North of England (map **A**).

During the Industrial Revolution, the North was the industrial powerhouse of the UK, and Manchester was the second largest city. In many parts of the North an industrial landscape was created, with mills and factories, railways and canals, terraced houses and chimneys belching out smoke and soot. Northern scenes were drawn by the artist L. S. Lowry, who became famous for his 'matchstick men' in the years after World War II. He painted a grim picture of life in the North (picture **B**).

There are plenty of people living in southeast England, who rarely, if ever, visit the North. What do they imagine it to be like? Look at map **C**. This is a **mental map**, not a real atlas map. Notice how the map is longer than the atlas map of England. Why? Because to many people in the South the North appears to be remote, to be further north than it really is. Some believe that it is not far from the North Pole!

N

NORTH OF ENGLAND

Hull

Humber estuary

Liverpool Manchester Sheffield

R. Mersey

R. Trent Nottingham

THE MIDLANDS

Birmingham

London

0 50 Miles

0 100 Kilometres

A The North of England

Key words

Economic – to do with money and wealth

Estuary – large mouth where a river goes into the sea.

Industrial Revolution – time of great factory growth from about 1750, based on using coal to make steam to drive new and bigger machinery

Mental map – mental maps show images of what people think.

B 'Industrial Landscape' by L. S. Lowry, 1955

D Images of the South East of England

THE SOUTH

In June 2003 the BBC showed a thirty-minute TV programme called *It's Grim Down South*. It made these points about London and the South East:

- High costs of housing: the average house in London costs over £200 000, twice the average for the UK.

- Long journeys to work: the average commuting time per day is two hours, again twice that in the rest of the country.

- Great overcrowding: cities are bursting at the seams; new housing estates are destroying green countryside all around them.

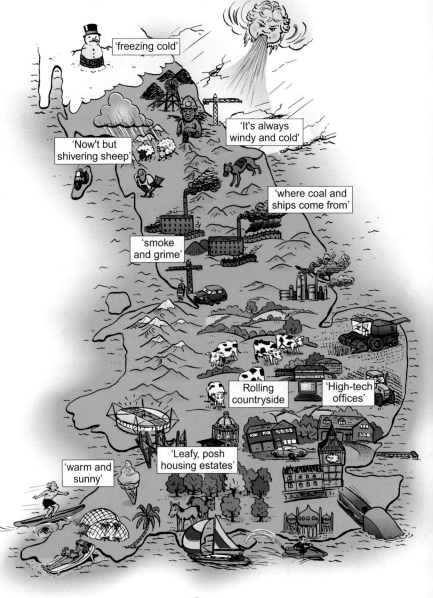

'freezing cold'

'Now't but shivering sheep'

'It's always windy and cold'

'where coal and ships come from'

'smoke and grime'

Rolling countryside

'High-tech offices'

'warm and sunny'

'Leafy, posh housing estates'

C Mental map of England

Activities

(S)

1 Look at map **C**.

a) Write down *two* ways in which a mental map is different from an atlas map.

b) What shows that some people in the South think that the North:

(i) has bad weather?

(ii) looks awful?

(iii) is a long way away?

c) Do you agree or disagree with these images of the North? Explain what you think.

2 Look at sketch **D** and write down what the sketch shows about the South East. Do you agree or disagree with these images? Explain what you think.

3 Work in groups to carry out your own class survey.

a) Ask each person in the group for their *main* image of the North and of the South East.

b) In your groups, draw sketches or mental maps of the North and South East to show what your classmates think.

The North–South divide: real or imagined?

>> **Learning to use data to make maps**
>> **Understanding evidence from a map to back up your ideas**

Photo **A** shows some northern graffiti. Obviously it is not true for everyone called Alison, but is it true for all places in the North of England? Photo **C** shows what used to be an old industrial and dock area near the centre of Manchester. Has Manchester changed from the time when Lowry painted it?

ECONOMIC DIFFERENCES IN THE UK

If the North–South divide is about differences in wealth, we need to look at some economic data. Map **B** shows the average amount people earn per week across the UK. Does the map provide any evidence for the North–South divide? Certainly it shows that people earn more money per week in the South East of England, and especially in London. But even London has its rich and poor areas. Photographs **D** and **E** were taken within 4 kilometres (2.5 miles) of each other in the East End of London.

A Northern graffiti

SKILLS

How to draw a shading map (also called a choropleth map)

1 Look at the highest and lowest values in your table of data, e.g. the highest and lowest wage.
2 Split the values up into four or five groups of equal size.
3 Choose a colour or type of shading for each group.
4 Very important – choose darker colours or denser shading for groups with high values.
5 Look at your data to see which areas on the map match the value groups you set up in step 2.
6 Shade or colour in each area correctly. Do not forget to add a key.

For more help, see page 124 of *SKILLS in Geography*

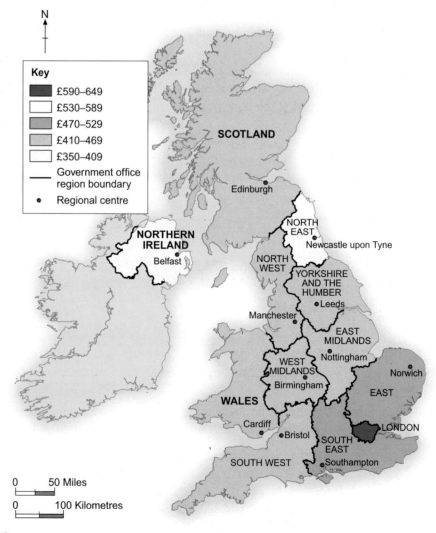

Key

	£590–649
	£530–589
	£470–529
	£410–469
	£350–409
——	Government office region boundary
•	Regional centre

B A shading map of the average weekly earnings in the UK (2003)

1. Look at map **B**. It has the four things that every good map should have. The first letters of these five things are T, K, N and S. Write out and complete these sentences:

   Every good map needs these five things. They are: 1 _____;
   2 _____; 3 _____; 4 _____

   (Look back to Chapter 2 page 16 if you need help.)

2. a) Make a frame and draw a sketch of photo **C**.

   b) Add at least *four* labels to show:

      (i) remains of the industrial past

      (ii) recent improvements.

3. Write down *two* differences between the housing in photographs **D** and **E**. Explain as fully as you can why photo **D** shows a wealthier area.

4. Using the table below, draw a choropleth map of average rates of unemployment in the UK. Follow the steps below and also look at the SKILLS box, page 54.

Average rates of unemployment in the UK in 2002 (%)			
North East	9.1	Yorkshire and the Humber	6.0
Scotland	7.6	North West	5.3
Northern Ireland	7.0	East Midlands	5.1
London	7.0	South West	4.1
West Midlands	6.2	East	3.6
Wales	6.1	South East	3.3

   a) Trace the outline map of administrative regions (map **D** on page 51).

   b) Make a key of colours or shading for these classes:

   | 2.0–3.9 | 4.0–5.9 | 6.0–7.9 | 8.0–9.9 |

   lightest colour or shading ⟶ darkest colour or shading

   c) Check that your map has the things that every good map needs.

   d) Exchange your map with that of the person sitting next to you. Mark their map out of 10. Follow the scheme below.

What to give marks for	Number of marks
Values (12) plotted accurately with correct colours or shading used ($\frac{1}{2}$ mark each)	6 marks
Good colour scheme or shading used	1 mark
Title and north sign included ($\frac{1}{2}$ mark each)	1 mark
Neatly drawn	1 mark
Good overall appearance	1 mark

5. Look at the map of unemployment you have drawn. Does it suggest that the North–South divide exists? Explain as fully as you can.

C Castlefields, next to the city centre of Manchester

D Expensive houses beside the Thames in East London

E A block of flats in Tower Hamlets, East London

London is different

> **Understanding how London is different**
> **Learning to use grids to find places on a map**

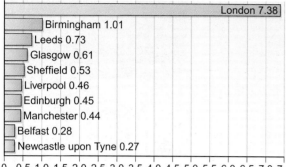

A Top ten cities in the UK (2001)

London is a big city. It is easily the UK's largest city, with almost 7.4 million inhabitants (**A**). This makes it seven times larger than Birmingham, the second largest city.

London is the capital of the UK. The Houses of Parliament are in Westminster (see page 45) and many government offices are on Whitehall, between the Houses of Parliament and Trafalgar Square (**B**). The Prime Minister lives in 10 Downing Street, a road off Whitehall.

London is a large financial centre. Only New York is larger. The Bank of England and the Stock Exchange are in that part of London known as 'the City'. Photo **C** was taken in the 'City' of London, a place of work little visited by tourists. This lies to the east of St Paul's Cathedral (see square H3 on map **E** opposite). More companies have their headquarters in London than in any other European city.

London has become one of the world's big tourist centres. The world's two most popular cities for tourists to visit are London and Paris. Of the top ten places for visitor numbers in the UK in 2001, six were in London (table **D**). Have you visited any of them? Can you spot one way that most of those located *out* of London are different from many of the ones *in* London?

Today it is London and not the North that is described as the 'engine which drives the rest of the country'. This is because of its great national and international importance.

B Trafalgar Square

C 'The City'

Rank	Attraction	Visitor (millions)	Free or paid entry
1	Blackpool Pleasure Beach, Blackpool, Lancashire	6.5	Free
2	National Gallery (art museum), London	4.9	Free
3	British Museum, London	4.8	Free
4	London Eye (giant wheel), London	3.9	Paid
5	Tate Modern (art museum), London	3.6	Free
6	Pleasureland Theme Park, Southport, Lancashire	2.1	Free
7	Tower of London, London	2.0	Paid
8	Clacton Pier, Clacton, Essex	1.8	Free
9	Eden Project, St Austell, Cornwall	1.7	Paid
10	Natural History Museum, London	1.7	Paid

D UK attractions with the most visitors (2001)

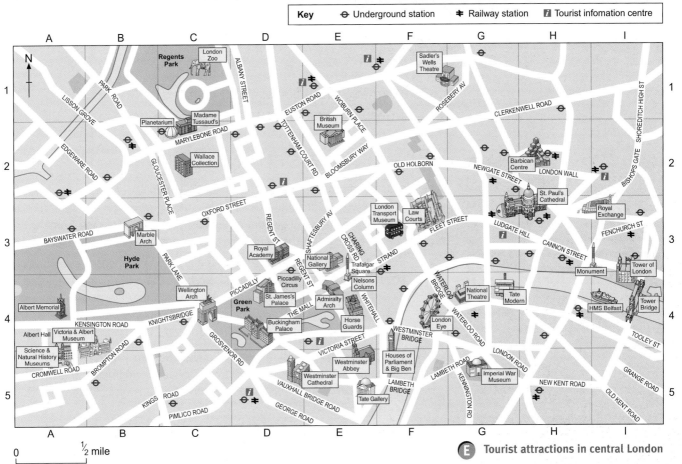

0 ——— ½ mile

E **Tourist attractions in central London**

Activities

1 a) Using **D**, draw a bar graph to show visitor numbers to the top ten UK attractions in 2001 (for more help see page 123 of *SKILLS in geography*).

b) Colour or shade in the bars of the attractions in London and finish the graph with a title and a key.

2 State *three* ways in which London is different from all the other UK cities.

3 Study map **E**.

a) Name the attraction in each of these map squares.

(i) A5   (ii) E3   (iii) F4   (iv) C1

b) Give the squares in which each of these is located:

(i) British Museum   (ii) Tate Modern.

c) Name one attraction for visitors in each of these map squares.

(i) B3   (ii) D4   (iii) E4   (iv) F5

d) What do the four attractions in c) have in common? Which is the odd one out? Now, try making up your own odd one out.

e) What is found in all these squares?

(i) A2   (ii) E1   (iii) D5   (iv) G4

Why are they important for visitors to London?

f) How many theatres are named on the map and which squares are they in?

4 Use a search engine on the Internet to find out more about one of the visitor attractions named in table **D**. Click on www.heinemann.co.uk/hotlinks and insert express code **6437P**.

Visitors' London

>> Learning about London as a visitor
>> Drawing a sketch map for a walking tour

OVERSEAS VISITORS

What do visitors from overseas come to see in London? A family living in London, who often have visitors from the USA to stay, recommend the following tourist 'hot spots' to their first-time visitors to London. They have learned from experience that these are the 'must see' places for Americans in London.

- Start at the London Eye (**A**). This is the giant wheel of space age pods on the south bank of the Thames. Built to celebrate the millennium, the Eye is a big hit with visitors. In good weather there are brilliant views all over London.

- Next cross Westminster Bridge, see Big Ben and the Houses of Parliament, and visit Westminster Abbey.

- Then walk up Whitehall to take in Trafalgar Square (Nelson's Column with lions and fountains), Leicester Square (theatres, cinemas and eating places) and Piccadilly Circus (flashy neon advertising signs and statue of Eros).

After this, it depends upon what the American visitors most want to do in London. If they are interested in the Royal Family, they are told to go to the Changing of the Guard at Buckingham Palace, or to Madame Tussauds to have their photographs taken next to the wax figures of the Queen and the rest of her family.

If history interests them, they are told to make for the Tower of London near Tower Bridge (photo **B**). It is no longer a place for chopping off the heads of enemies, as it was when the UK was ruled by kings and queens. On days that are too wet or cold for sightseeing, they visit the museums. When it is time to shop, they find their way to Selfridges in Oxford Street and to other shopping streets in the West End, such as Regent Street and Bond Street, or take the tube to Harrods in Knightsbridge.

A The London Eye

B Tower Bridge

Most overseas visitors expect to see red telephone boxes, black taxi cabs and red double-decker buses that they can hop on and hop off. This is because they have seen them on the movies and TV shows.

Many visitors enjoy the quirks – the crazy differences between the UK and anywhere else in the world. For example, they like hearing the warning 'Mind the Gap' on the London Underground. Many of them try 'pub grub', including 'bangers and mash' and 'sticky toffee pudding'.

BRITISH VISITORS

People come to London from all over Britain for many of the same reasons and to see the same popular sights. However, Christmas shoppers and bargain hunters in the January sales are more likely to be British than American or French. Special events such as Trooping the Colour (in June) and the London Marathon (in April) attract large crowds. Major sporting events are held all over London: Wembley (football), Wimbledon (tennis), Lord's (cricket) and Twickenham (rugby football).

C Central London

Activities

1   Look at photo **C**. You are going to make a labelled sketch.

   a) Make a frame and draw a sketch of what can be seen (see page 125 of *SKILLS in geography* for more help).

   b) Add labels to show features of interest for overseas visitors to London.

2   Write down what attracts visitors to each of these places in London:

   a) Oxford Street   b) Leicester Square   c) Piccadilly Circus

   d) Buckingham Palace   e) Trafalgar Square   f) Wembley

   g) Westminster   h) Knightsbridge

3   Why does London attract visitors at all times of the year? Explain as fully as you can.

4   Two visitors went on a walking tour of London, starting and ending at the London Eye. Their route was:

   London Eye ⟶ Westminster and Big Ben ⟶ Trafalgar Square ⟶ St Paul's Cathedral ⟶ Tower of London ⟶ Tower Bridge ⟶ Tate Modern ⟶ London Eye.

   a) Using map **E** on page 57, make your own sketch map to show the route they followed.

   b) Show and label the places they visited.

5   Imagine visitors were coming to your home area. In groups make a list of the places for them to visit and things to do. Provide as much information as possible about the places you list, such as prices, opening times and locations. For more help, visit your local tourist information centre. Finish off by producing a visitor brochure with photographs and pictures on the computer.

Football is countrywide

>> **Understanding what football can teach us about geography**
>> **Learning to draw pie graphs**

N
Newcastle
Middlesbrough
Blackburn
Leeds
Bolton
Liverpool
Everton
Manchester United
Manchester City
Wolves
Leicester
Birmingham City
Aston Villa
Arsenal
Charlton Athletic
Chelsea
Fulham
Tottenham
Southampton
Portsmouth
Key
Football club
0 50 Miles
0 100 Kilometres

A Premiership Clubs in the season 2003–4

More people follow football than any other sport in the UK. British football teams also have a huge following in other parts of the world, especially in the Far East and Australia. Manchester United is one of the world's best-known club teams. However, in some of the most remote places in the world you will meet people who have heard of Sheffield Wednesday, Notts County and Leyton Orient, without having any idea where the clubs play and why they have these 'strange' names.

PREMIERSHIP CLUBS

Which clubs have moved in and out of the Premiership League since May 2004? What does map **A** show about the locations of Premiership clubs in the 2003–4 season?

The clubs are well spread out.

The greatest distance for players and supporters to travel by road is 545 kilometres (340 miles). Between which two clubs is this?

All the big cities have at least one team.

Is this true? Look back at graph A on page 56. There are seven English cities in the graph. Is there a city without a team in the Premier league?

B Arsenal's first-team squad in 2003–4

The large Premiership Clubs are rich from television money and from playing in European competitions like the Champions League. They can afford to buy and pay some of the world's best players. There are many players from overseas. This means that the big clubs like Arsenal and Manchester United are **multi-racial** and **multi-national** (photo **B** and table **C**).

LEAGUE CLUBS IN DIVISIONS 1–3

These clubs are the poor relations of those in the Premiership. However, they are much more widely distributed throughout England and Wales. Look at map **D**. Which club do you think will spend most on travelling to play other clubs during the season?

Although these clubs are less well known, each one has a hard core of devoted fans. Clubs often receive support from local businesses and the council, because having a team in the football league brings publicity. The name of the town is read out on radio and TV with the scores and is in the sports pages of all the Sunday papers.

Country	Number of players	Country	Number of players
UK	12	Portugal	1
France	3	South Africa	1
Republic of Ireland	2	Spain	1
Brazil	1	The Netherlands	1
Cameroon	1	Uruguay	1
Norway	1	USA	1

Source: Taken from player profiles on the Manchester United website

C Countries where players in the Manchester United first team squad were born (August 2003)

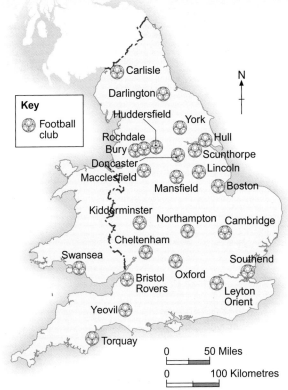

Key
- Football club

D Third Division Clubs in the season 2003–4

Activities

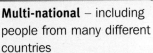

1 a) Make a table like the one below. Give it the title 'Number of football teams in each region, 2003–4'. Using maps **A** and **D**, fill in the number of teams in each region.

	London	South	Midlands	North	Wales
Premiership					
Division 3					

b) (i) Which part of England has most clubs for both leagues?

(ii) Can you think of any possible reason for this?

(iii) Third Division clubs are more widely spread throughout the country than Premiership Clubs. What shows this? Answer as fully as you can.

2 Choose *either* Manchester United *or* your favourite football league club. On an outline world map, shade in and name the countries where their players were born.

3 a) Why have the big clubs become multi-national teams?

b) Think about and write down *one* advantage and *one* disadvantage of teams being multi-national.

4 Name the football league club closest to you. Find out some information about it, for example: where the ground is, whether all the players come from the UK, how big the crowds are. Make a presentation to your class using ICT or on paper.

5 Look at the table you made in activity 1. Using your computer, create two pie graphs (see the SKILLS box), one to show the Premiership teams and one to show the Third Division teams for each area.

Key words
Multi-national – including people from many different countries
Multi-racial – including people from many racial groups

SKILLS

How to draw a pie graph
1 If necessary, turn the figures you are using into percentages.
2 Multiply each percentage by 3.6° (100 per cent = 360°), for example: 1 per cent = 3.6°; 10 per cent = 36°
3 Draw a circle.
4 Start at the top (12 o'clock).
5 Plot the segments (usually largest to smallest). Draw lines from the centre of the circle to the edge to show the different-sized segments.

For more help, see page 122 of *SKILLS in geography*

What is the UK?

What do you know about Britain? Around Britain Quiz

1 Work in teams to do this map quiz. Look at the sentences A–J below. They give some well-known facts about places in Britain. For each sentence, use an atlas to find the name of the place it describes. (For more help on using an atlas, see page 121 of *SKILLS in geography*.)

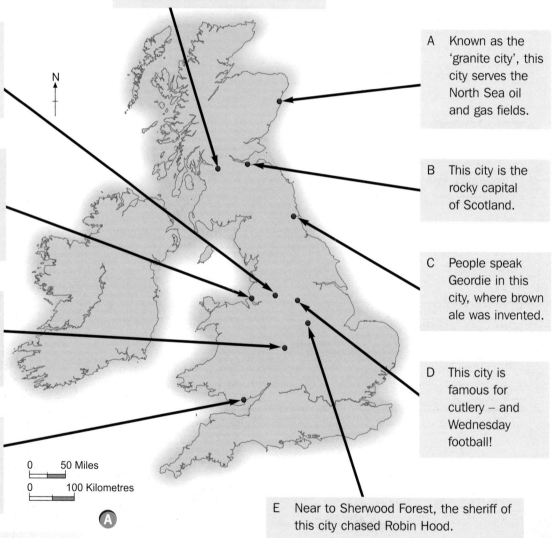

J The largest city in Scotland, where Rangers and Celtic are rival football teams.

I In this northern city you will find Coronation Street and Old Trafford.

H The Beatles were born in this port city, which will be the European City of Culture in 2008.

F This is the UK's second city, with a Bull Ring and the National Exhibtion Centre.

G The Millennium Stadium is a showpiece in this Welsh capital.

A Known as the 'granite city', this city serves the North Sea oil and gas fields.

B This city is the rocky capital of Scotland.

C People speak Geordie in this city, where brown ale was invented.

D This city is famous for cutlery – and Wednesday football!

E Near to Sherwood Forest, the sheriff of this city chased Robin Hood.

N

0   50 Miles

0   100 Kilometres

What did you know?

2 Swap answers with another team. Mark their answers while the teacher calls the correct answers out. How did you all do?

3 Talk about the facts that surprised you. Were they often about places a long way from where you live?

» 5   Moving goods and people around

Container ships are one of the ways that goods are transported around the world today.

What do you know about transport links within and outside the UK?

Learning objectives

What are you going to learn about in this chapter?

> The pattern of trunk roads in Great Britain

> The importance of road transport and the problems it causes

> Why travel by rail is now less important than travel by road

> Increasing global links by air and sea between the UK and the rest of the world

 A container ship at Hong Kong

Britain's trunk roads

>> **Understanding the pattern of trunk roads in Britain**
>> **Identifying A-class roads and motorways**

WHAT IS A TRUNK ROAD?

If this was a joke in a Christmas cracker, the obvious answer would be 'A road for elephants'! However, in Britain, the main **A-class roads** and **motorways** in Britain are called **trunk roads**. Trunk roads are the busiest and most important roads that link large British towns and cities. They were built to take heavy traffic and carry about 36 per cent of all road traffic.

THE MAIN A-CLASS ROADS

A-class roads are the old roads between places, built long before motorways were invented. Some follow sections of old Roman roads. They all follow routes used by horse-drawn coaches before the coming of the railways in the mid-nineteenth century. A-class roads have been important lines of movement for centuries, whereas motorways have existed in Britain for less than 50 years.

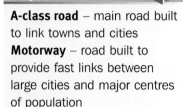

Key words

A-class road – main road built to link towns and cities
Motorway – road built to provide fast links between large cities and major centres of population
Trunk road – road built for heavy traffic

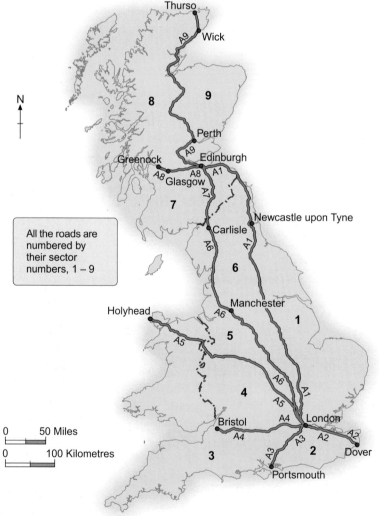

All the roads are numbered by their sector numbers, 1 – 9

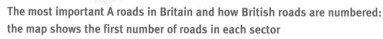

A The most important A roads in Britain and how British roads are numbered: the map shows the first number of roads in each sector

WHERE ARE BRITAIN'S MOTORWAYS?

Motorways are modern roads. They were built where demand for moving people and goods by car, bus, van and lorry was greatest. Therefore they are found in greatest numbers and are closest together in areas of high population. The main purpose of motorways is to move goods and people long distances, as quickly and easily as possible. Except for a few which lead into city centres, it is deliberate policy to keep motorways out of built-up areas. This helps to keep traffic away from people.

Notice that the motorways follow the same numbering system as the A-roads. For example, the M6, M62 and M65 are all in road sector 6.

Look at map **A**. Which road sector do you live in?

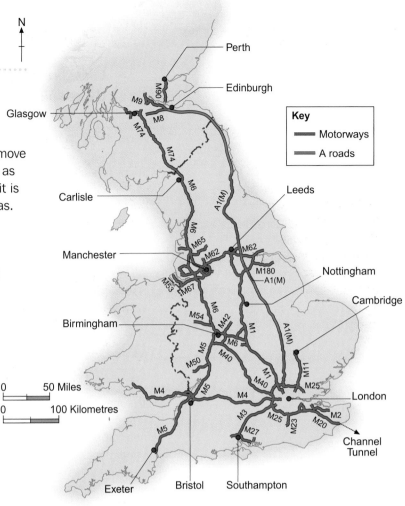

B Motorways in Great Britain

Activities

1   Using map **A**, make a table like the one below and fill it in for roads A1 to A9.

Road	From	To
A1		
A2		

2   'The main A-class roads in England and Wales are like the spokes of a bicycle wheel. London is in the wheel hub and roads radiate out from it'.

   a) Look at map **A**. Draw a diagram or sketch map to show how the main A-class trunk roads go out from London 'like the spokes of a bicycle wheel'.

   b) Now do the same to show the pattern of trunk roads in Scotland.

3   Look at the OS map of your local area.

   a) Give examples of A roads and motorways (if there are any).

   b) Name the places each road passes through.

   c) What shows that the A roads and motorways are more important than other roads? Answer as fully as you can.

4   a) Find the M25 on map **B**. State *one* difference between it and the other motorways.

   b) The M25 is a very busy motorway. Can you explain why?

5   **Motorway quiz – Name the motorway!**

   Work with a partner. Using maps **A** and **B**, make up *ten* questions for a motorway quiz, then use them to test another pair. Here are some questions that a pair of students made up.

   1   Which motorway links Manchester and Leeds? (Answer: M62)

   2   You are going on holiday to France using the Channel Tunnel. Which motorway will you use? (Answer: M20)

Moving goods around Britain by road

>> **Considering the delivery of goods by road**
>> **Using spider diagrams**

Key words

Congestion – too much traffic using the road at the same time
Logistics – organising the movement of goods (and sometimes people)

Have you seen the word **Logistics** written on the side of a lorry or delivery van? It used to be the military word for the art of supplying and providing for armies. Today it is used by many road delivery companies, transporting:

- food to supermarkets
- machinery and parts to factories
- equipment to offices
- goods to people's homes, bought from catalogues or through the Internet.

Some companies offer delivery within 24 hours, many within 48 or 72 hours. Without motorways, they could not offer these fast deliveries.

WHAT ARE THE PROBLEMS WITH MOTORWAYS?

The main problem is **congestion**. It is estimated that 20 per cent of the motorway network suffers from heavy congestion on at least three days a week. Motorways near urban areas are blocked at rush hours every working day. Roadworks or a minor accident can cause tailbacks of ten miles or more. Vehicles slowing down, stopping and starting use extra fuel and cause more air pollution (diagram **A**).

Not everyone thinks that building new lanes for motorways eases congestion (**B**). They believe that 'traffic increases to fill the space available'. However, in 2002 the UK government indicated that extra lanes might be added to the busiest stretches of motorway, such as the M6 between Manchester and Birmingham. The M6 carries 160 000 vehicles a day, although it was built for only 72 000. The first toll motorway in the UK opened in 2003 to relieve congestion on the M6 around Birmingham (see the M6 Toll website at www.heinemann.co.uk/hotlinks).

Extra lanes have already been added on certain sections of the M25. A second road bridge was built across the River Severn in 1996 (map **C**).

carbon dioxide, sulphur dioxide, black smoke and particulates, carbon monoxide and nitrogen oxides

> It will cause traffic chaos while the work is being done.

> It will not solve congestion when it is finished because traffic will increase.

> The billions of pounds it will cost would be better spent on other things.

A Up the nose: what comes out of vehicle exhaust pipes

B Some opinions about widening motorways

C OS map showing part of the Severn estuary, scale 1:50 000

metres   kilometres

Activities

1 Find square 5485 on map **C**.

  a) Draw and name as many different symbols to do with transport as you can find in this square.

  b) Why are there so many of them in this square?

2 a) Make a frame that is the same size as OS map **C**.

  b) Draw in the grid lines and mark on the courses of the motorways and the A-class roads.

  c) Show and label the bridges and motorway junctions.

3 The bridge marked *Severn Road Bridge* was built first.

  a) What is the direction of travel from Wales to England over the bridge?

  b) State the length in kilometres of:

    (i) that part of the bridge across the River Severn

    (ii) the whole length of the bridge across both rivers.

  c) Why do you think the bridge was built at this point and not further south?

4 The new bridge marked M4 is different in several ways from the old bridge. Write down as many differences as you can find between the two bridges.

5 ***Advantages and disadvantages of motorways***

Work in pairs. Draw larger versions of these spider diagrams. Add more examples of advantages and disadvantages of motorways.

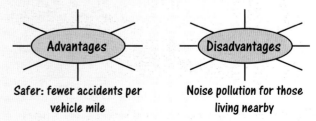

Safer: fewer accidents per vehicle mile

Noise pollution for those living nearby

© Crown copyright. Licence no. 100000230

How important is road travel?

>> **Comparing road and rail travel**

>> **Learning how to draw block graphs**

Key words

Freight – goods transported by water, land and air

Pipeline – goods flowing continuously through a pipe, such as water, gas and oil

To understand the importance of road travel, look first at graphs **A** and **B**. They show how passengers and **freight** were moved around Britain in 2000. Observe how methods of road transport dominate in both graphs, especially for passenger movements. What percentage of passenger movements was *not* by road in 2000?

Next look at graph **C**. It shows the trends in freight movements in Britain over the 40 years from 1955 to 1995. The figures for 1955 are interesting, because in that year almost the same amounts of goods were moved by rail and by road. What has happened since 1955 to road transport compared with rail? What would you expect the values in 2005 to show?

WHY HAS ROAD TRAFFIC INCREASED SO MUCH?

The main reason is increased car ownership. In 1952 only 15 per cent of households in Britain had regular use of a car. Fifty years later, in 2002, this had jumped to 73 per cent. The private car allows freedom of movement on a scale never previously imagined.

Moving from place to place, by road, rail and air, has never been easier than it is easier today. Did you know that the average British person in 2001:

- travelled about 11 000 kilometres (6500 miles)
- made just over 1000 trips in the year
- spent 360 hours travelling (= 15 days)?

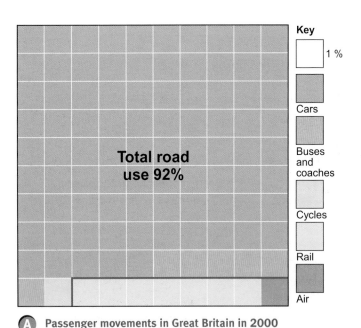

A Passenger movements in Great Britain in 2000

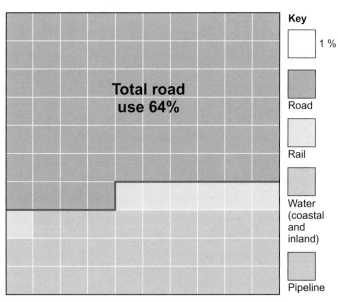

B Freight transport in Great Britain in 2000

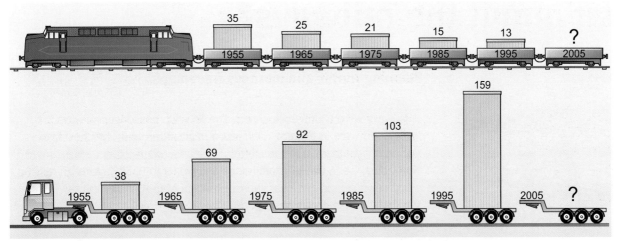

C Rail freight and road freight in Great Britain (billion tonne kilometres 1955–1995)

Activities

1 Draw a block graph to show the percentages in table **D** (see the SKILLS box). Finish it off with a title and a key.

2 Look at graphs **A–C**. Make a bullet point list of statistics to show that road transport is more important than rail transport. One example is given as a starter.

- *Passenger movements   92 per cent by road, 7 per cent by rail*

3 *Class activity – How important is road transport?*

a) Each person should make a recording sheet like the one started below. Fill it in for one week.

Journeys made by all methods of transport in one week				
Day of the week	**Journey from:**	**Journey to:**	**Method of transport**	**Time taken**

b) At the end of the week, each person adds up the total time they spent using each of the different methods of transport. Draw a bar graph to show the total times (see *SKILLS in geography* page 123).

c) Next add up the class totals and draw another graph.

d) Is road transport very important for people in your class? Explain as fully as you can. Is the pattern in your class similar to that for the whole country? If not, why not? Think about the type of area you live in.

Type	Percentage
Cars	81
Light vans	9
Goods vehicles (lorries)	7
Motor cycles	2
Pedal cycles	1

D Road traffic in Great Britain by vehicle type, 2000

SKILLS

How to draw a block graph

1 Make a grid of 100 squares.
2 One square equals 1 per cent.
3 Choose a different shade or colour for each value.
4 Shade or colour in the number of squares for the percentage.
5 Make a key for the shading or colours used.

For more help see page 123 of *SKILLS in geography*

What about the railways?

>> Looking at the decline (drop) in rail travel
>> Planning routes and journeys from maps

Railways were a British invention. The first two passenger railways in the world were in Britain – Darlington to Stockton and Manchester to Liverpool. Both were in the North of England, where steam engines had previously been used in coal mines and works to haul wagons on rails up and down slopes and over short distances. Map **A** shows the rail system in 1914, when it was at its peak.

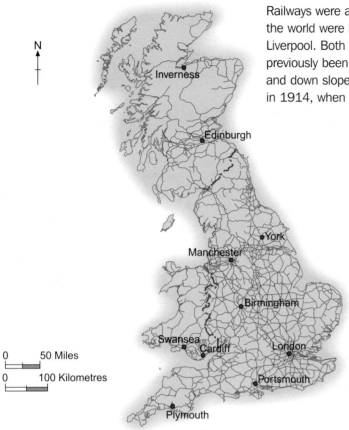

N

0 ____ 50 Miles

0 ____ 100 Kilometres

A The rail system in 1914

Key words

Economic – to do with money or making money
Environmental – affecting the natural surroundings (such as air, water, land, habitats and wildlife)
Heavy goods – bulky goods usually used by industries (such as coal, oil and rocks)

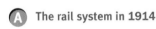

B Comparing the length of roads and rail track in the UK (2001)

(Bar chart: Length (thousand km) — Rail track 32000, Road 392000)

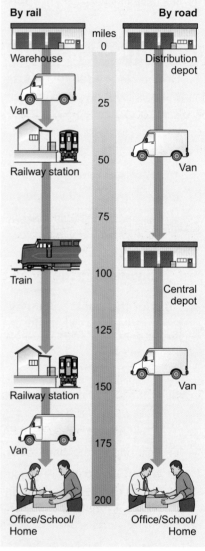

By rail | **By road**

miles
0

Warehouse — Distribution depot
Van
25
Railway station — Van
50
Train
75
Central depot
100
125
Railway station — Van
150
Van
175
Office/School/Home — Office/School/Home
200

C Transporting a package by rail and road

WHY ARE ONLY 7 PER CENT OF GOODS MOVED BY RAIL TODAY?

Graph **B** shows one reason. The length of rail track in Britain is less than 10 per cent of that of roads. Roads go everywhere, whereas many places are miles from the nearest station. Diagram **C** illustrates a second reason. It is more difficult to send a package by rail than by road. Can you understand why delivery companies do not use trains?

Over half the goods moved by rail are **heavy goods**. These are bulky products, such as minerals and metals, for which transport by rail has both **economic** and **environmental** advantages.

Map **D** shows the passenger railway network in the UK in 2003. There are a few other lines that are used just for freight. Can you describe the difference between this map and map **A**?

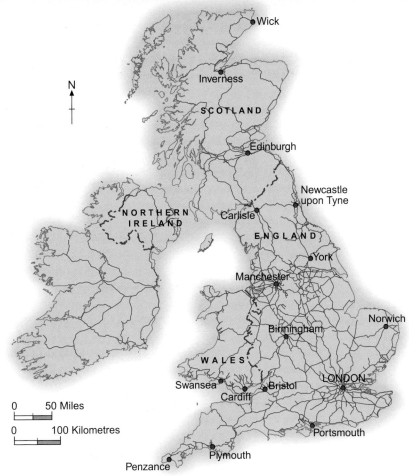

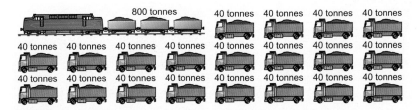

D Passenger railway network in the UK in 2003

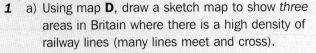

E Two ways to carry 800 tonnes of coal: one train but how many lorries?

Activities

1 a) Using map **D**, draw a sketch map to show *three* areas in Britain where there is a high density of railway lines (many lines meet and cross).

   b) Choose *one* of them. Why are there many railway lines?

2 a) Look at the rail website at www.heinemann.co.uk/hotlinks. Plan a route for a family going from Bolton in Lancashire to Gatwick Airport, without passing through London. Name the main stations they would pass through.

   b) Describe one possible route for a student travelling from Norwich in East Anglia to Holyhead in North Wales.

   c) (i) Look at map **D** and an atlas. Between which two places is the longest direct rail journey in Britain?

   (ii) Describe a possible route between these two places.

3 Visit the National Rail website: click on www.heinemann.co.uk/hotlinks and insert express code **6437P**. Plan a journey of at least 160 kilometres (100 miles) to a seaside resort. Give details of the route, where to change trains and the time taken.

4 Look at **E**. Think about as many advantages of carrying coal by train as you can. Write them down.

Global links: from the UK to other countries

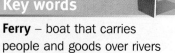

Key words

Ferry – boat that carries people and goods over rivers and short sea crossings
Global – worldwide, throughout the world

>> **Understanding transport links between the UK and other parts of the world**
>> **Looking at the importance of air travel**

The UK is an island country. This has always made travelling to another country more difficult – before air travel, a boat journey was always needed. **Ferry** links remain very important today, as in every island country. Dover to Calais is the busiest ferry link with mainland Europe, because the Channel crossing here is the shortest – only 33 kilometres (21 miles).

TRAVELLING TO OTHER COUNTRIES HAS NEVER BEEN EASIER

Cars and passengers going to mainland Europe, as well as lorries carrying freight, now have three options. They can either go by ferry, or use the rail service through the Channel Tunnel between Folkestone and Calais.

The third option is travel by air. It takes only minutes for planes to fly people and cargo goods over the English Channel and North Sea to Europe. Flying from one of London's airports, it is possible for people, whether on holiday or on business, to reach most countries in the world in a day.

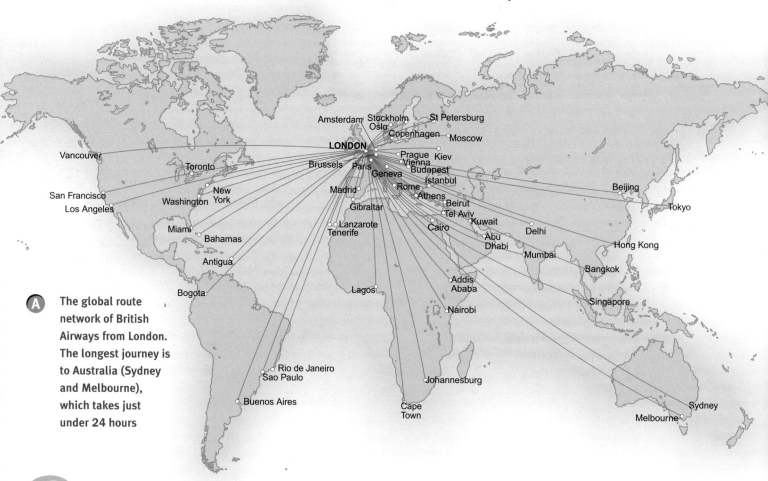

A The global route network of British Airways from London. The longest journey is to Australia (Sydney and Melbourne), which takes just under 24 hours

THE GROWTH OF AIR TRAVEL

The number of people carried into and out of UK airports trebled in the 20 years between 1981 and 2001. The amount of freight moved by air more than doubled. The government thinks these trends will continue. It expects the number of air passengers to grow by 5 per cent per year and freight by 7 per cent.

Look at map **B**. What does the map show about the importance of airports in London and the South East?

Did you know that in 2003:

- Heathrow was the world's busiest airport for international travellers
- Gatwick had the world's busiest single runway
- Stansted was the fastest growing airport in Europe?

Much of the growth at Stansted was due to the success of low-cost airlines, such as Easyjet and Ryanair, in attracting passengers for travel within the UK and Europe.

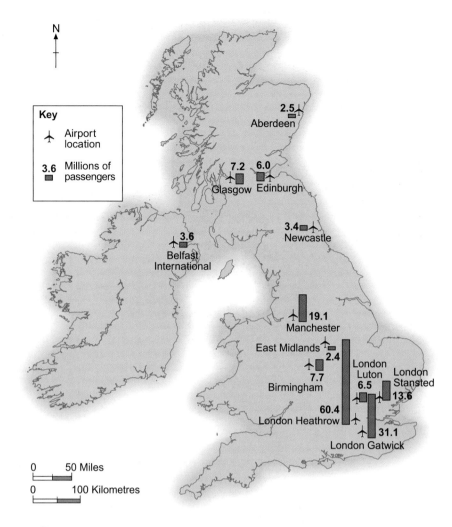

Key

✈ Airport location

3.6 ■ Millions of passengers

0 ___ 50 Miles

0 ___ 100 Kilometres

B The UK's top twelve airports for passengers, 2001

Activities ⓢ

1. a) Draw a bar graph to show passenger numbers in 2001 at the top twelve UK airports.

   b) Shade or colour in the bars for:
      - London airports
      - Other English airports
      - Scottish and Irish airports.

      Make a key. For more help, go to page 00 of SKILLS.

2. a) How many passengers used the four London airports in 2001?

   b) The total number of passengers in all UK airports in 2001 was 180 million.

      (i) What percentage used Heathrow and Gatwick?

      (ii) Draw a pie graph to show these percentages.

   c) Write a short paragraph starting 'London's airports are some of the busiest in the world because ...'

3. 'Low-flying aircraft pass over many parts of south and west London every 30 seconds at peak times, disrupting conversation by day and sleep by night.'

   a) Name the problem.

   b) Think of another disadvantage of living near an airport.

   c) Are there any advantages? Explain your answer.

4. People say: 'The world is shrinking'. Give reasons why it has become much easier to reach:

   a) other European countries

   b) distant places like Asia and Australia.

Global links: between other countries and the UK

>> **Introducing globalisation**
>> **Finding out where goods come from**

T-shirt made in Indonesia

Trousers from Vietnam

Trainers made in Thailand

A Global clothing!

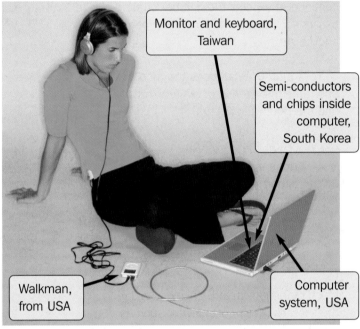

Monitor and keyboard, Taiwan

Semi-conductors and chips inside computer, South Korea

Walkman, from USA

Computer system, USA

B Global electronics

Global links are increasing. It is all part of **globalisation**. The UK is not an isolated island, unaffected by what is happening in the rest of the world. Goods are imported from countries in all six inhabited continents. The UK imports:

- **raw materials** (such as minerals and timber)
- foodstuffs (such as bananas and rice)
- **manufactured goods** (such as clothes and cars).

GOING GLOBAL

You are examples of *global man* and *global woman*! Did you know that? Look at the labelling on your clothes and on electronic goods at home. How many have 'Made in Britain' on the label?

Although Nike has offices in the UK (**C**), most of the clothes and trainers they sell here are made in the Far East. This is why Nike is an example of a **multi-national** company – it operates in many countries of the world (map **D**).

High wages are the main reason why factories are not located in the UK and Europe. Costs of living are much lower in the Far East, and so are wages. The rate of pay per hour is often less than 10 per cent of that in the UK, yet the workers there have equal skills. There used to be more factories in Hong Kong, Singapore and South Korea; however, as wage rates increased, companies switched production to less wealthy countries.

Key words

Container – a closed metal box for transporting goods by road, rail and sea
Globalisation – countries, people and companies are becoming more and more international
Manufactured goods – things that are made, usually in a factory
Multi-national company – one that has offices and factories in many countries
Raw materials – natural resources used for making other things

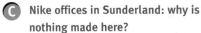

C Nike offices in Sunderland: why is nothing made here?

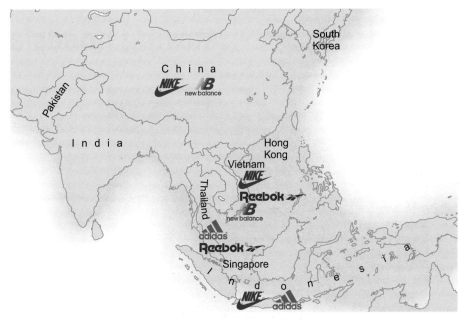

D Where multi-national companies have their factories

TRANSPORTING TRAINERS FROM THE FAR EAST TO THE UK

The cheapest way to transport goods long distances is by sea. Most manufactured goods are packed in **containers** (see box **E**) and transported on giant container ships (see page 63), which arrive about two weeks later in the UK. Some use the Suez Canal, while others travel around the Cape of Good Hope in South Africa.

Activities

S

1 Look at labelling – on your clothes, on the foods you eat and on goods in the home.

a) Make a table like the one below. List places of origin for at least *four* of each type.

	Foods	Clothes	Goods in the home
1			
2			

b) On an outline map of the world, shade and name the countries in your table.

c) Design a poster with the heading either *Global Man* or *Global Woman* using some of the items from your table.

2 Using map **D** and box **E**, write about the advantages of moving goods in containers.

3 On a world outline map, plot the routes that container ships use from the Far East to the UK.

4 Can you think of *two* advantages and *two* disadvantages of locating factories in the Far East?

- Metal boxes of standard sizes and shapes
- Packed and sealed in the factory or warehouse
- Can be transferred between different types of transport (lorries, trains and ships)
- Easily lifted on and off different types of transport by cranes
- Only unsealed and opened at their final destination

E About containers

Moving goods and people around

A A logistics company van

Setting up a distribution and delivery company

You have been asked to help set up a company to deliver parcels by road to customers throughout Great Britain within 48 hours. It must be well located for the motorways.

Stage 1: Choose a location for the Head Office

1 Think about *two* or *three* possible locations. List their advantages. Look at map **B** showing major motorways to help you.

You might wish to consider these factors before making the decision:
- shortest distances to all parts of Great Britain
- nearness to large cities
- within easy reach of major motorways.

2 Decide upon the location with most advantages. Write *two* or *three* sentences explaining why you have chosen that location.

Stage 2: Pick a name for the company and design its logo

3 Try to find a name that is likely to appeal to customers.

4 Design a logo that will look good on the sides of the vans and be a good advertisement for the company.

Stage 3: Plan two of the busy delivery routes from your Head Office

5 List the motorways used to reach these destinations.
  a) Route 1 – from Head Office to one of the big English cities (e.g. London, Birmingham or Manchester).
  b) Route 2 – from Head Office to a city in Scotland.

Stage 4: Plan a route for a special parcel delivery to Paris

6 Use a search engine on the Internet to find the best route to France from your Head Office. Click on www.heinemann.co.uk/hotlinks and insert express code **6437P**.

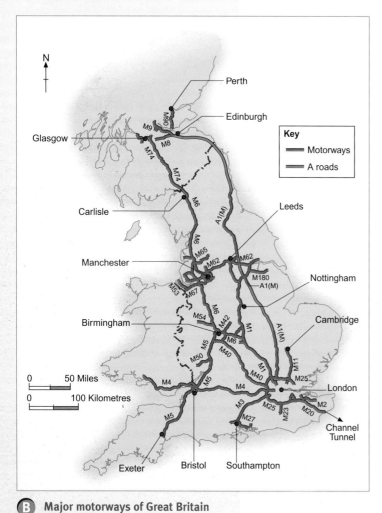

B Major motorways of Great Britain

»6 Great British scenery

The UK does not have mighty mountain ranges, big rivers and active volcanoes. What it does have is some of the world's best coastal scenery. Why are these cliffs so high and steep? Why are they so white? Why are they called 'the *Seven* Sisters'?

Learning objectives

What are you going to learn about in this chapter?

> Coastal landforms and how to recognise them
> How wave erosion and weathering cause cliff collapse
> What can be done about Britain's crumbling cliffs
> Beaches and other landforms of deposition
> Britain's National Parks and their attractive landscapes
> How Carboniferous limestone produces distinctive scenery
> Limestone quarrying

 The Seven Sisters, East Sussex

Britain's coastal scenery

>> **Recognising coastal landforms**

>> **Understanding how the coast has been shaped by erosion**

If you have been to the seaside you will know at least some of the coastal **landforms** that are studied in geography. Perhaps the two best known coastal landforms are **cliffs** (page 77) and **beaches** (photograph **A**). Can you give geographical definitions for these terms? What is the beach in **A** made of? Where does the beach end?

RECOGNISING COASTAL LANDFORMS

You are less likely to know the names of other coastal landforms. For example, you might have walked out onto flat rocks when the tide was out, looking for crabs. Did you know you were walking across a **wave-cut platform**? It is important to be able to recognise and name landforms from photographs, diagrams and maps. The next time you go to the coast, you should be able to name all the landforms.

Look at cross-section **B** and compare it with photograph **C**. The flatter area below the loose rocks at the bottom of the chalk cliffs is the wave-cut platform. There are two signs in **C** that the cliff collapse was recent. What are they?

A The beach at Bamburgh in Northumberland

Headlands are places where the coastline sticks out into the sea, often with strong, high cliffs. At the bottom of the cliffs, **caves** are common. Where the waves manage to cut through the headland, a natural **arch** forms. Sometimes an area of rock is cut off completely; this isolated piece of rock is called a **stack**. Later it may be eroded to sea level or below, when it is called a *stump*.

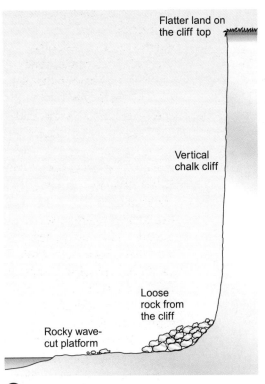

Flatter land on the cliff top

Vertical chalk cliff

Loose rock from the cliff

Rocky wave-cut platform

B Cross-section

C Chalk cliffs near Beachy Head in Sussex

 D Coastal landforms of erosion

 E Cave, arch and stack at Flamborough Head

All these landforms have been formed by **erosion** (**D**). Rock on the land was worn away by the force of the waves. Land has been lost. The coastline has retreated – it is now further back than it used to be. This can be a great problem for people with houses on cliff tops, as you will soon discover.

Activities   (S) (A)

1 Make a large table like the one below. Copy out what is shown for *arch*. Complete it in the same way for these six landforms:

> **cave   beach   cliff   headland   stack   wave-cut platform**

Coastal landforms		
Name of landform	**Written definition**	**Sketch to show its appearance**
Arch	Rocky opening through a headland	
Cave		

2 Look at photograph **E**. What do you think will happen to the arch in the future?

3 a) You are going to make a wordsearch box for the nine key words on this page.

- Make it 15 squares by 15 squares.
- Start with WAVECUTPLATFORM along one of the edges.
- Fit in the other eight key words.
- Fill in the spaces with other letters.

b) Swap it with your neighbour's wordsearch. See who finds the nine words first.

c) Test each other on the definitions of the nine words.

Key words

Arch – rocky opening through a headland

Beach – area of deposited material (for example, sand and shingle) between the high and low tide marks

Cave – hollow below the cliffs

Cliff – steep rock outcrop along a coast

Erosion – wearing away of the Earth's surface by rivers, waves and ice

Headland – where rock extends further out to sea than the rocks on either side

Landform – physical feature of the Earth's surface

Stack – pillar of rock surrounded by sea

Wave-cut platform – gently sloping area of rock below the beach, seen only at low tide

Britain's collapsing cliffs

>> Finding out how waves erode cliffs
>> Understanding how freeze–thaw weathering works

HOW DO WAVES ERODE ROCKS?

Cliffs are mainly formed by wave erosion (diagram **B**). There are two main processes.

- **Abrasion**: As the waves break, they throw sand and pebbles with sharp edges against the rock face of the cliff. Over time, these break off pieces of rock and cause undercutting at the bottom of the cliff.

- **Hydraulic action**: Water is heavy. The great weight and force of water breaking against the rock weakens it.

The greatest cliff collapses occur during **storms**. Strong winds whip up the waves. Hundreds of tonnes of water, loaded with sand and pebbles, can hit the rock face hard and at great speed. Cliffs made of soft rocks like clay can be eroded back by up to three metres (ten feet) in a big storm. The unexpected collapse of the Holbeck Hall Hotel in Scarborough in 1993 is a reminder of what can happen (photograph **A**).

A Collapse of the Holbeck Hall Hotel on Scarborough's South Cliff, June 1993

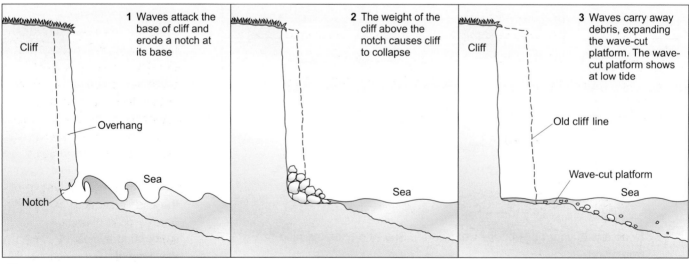

Cliff

1 Waves attack the base of cliff and erode a notch at its base

Overhang

Sea

Notch

2 The weight of the cliff above the notch causes cliff to collapse

Sea

Cliff

3 Waves carry away debris, expanding the wave-cut platform. The wave-cut platform shows at low tide

Old cliff line

Wave-cut platform

Sea

B How cliffs are formed by wave erosion

WEATHERING OF ROCKS

It is never totally safe to walk along the bottom of a cliff, even in good weather. The top of the cliff can collapse at any time because it has been weakened by **weathering**. A type of weathering called **freeze–thaw** is widespread in the UK (see **C**). It happens most in rocks with many cracks, like the one in photograph **D**. Water expands when it freezes, in rocks or anywhere else. This is why pipes burst during very cold spells of weather. The water in the pipe freezes and expands, splitting the pipe. When the weather warms up, the ice melts and water pours out through the split.

1 A crack in the rock fills with water.

Water trapped inside cracks in rocks expands as it freezes.

2 This puts pressure on the rock around it and the crack becomes wider.

3 Thawing releases the pressure.

After freezing and thawing is repeated many times, pieces of rock break off.

Eventually the crack gets so wide that the rock splits.

 How freeze–thaw works

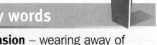 **Freeze–thaw is partly to blame for this rock fall. Why did it happen here?**

Activities

1 Look at photograph **A**. Draw a sketch to show what has happened. Why do cliffs collapse? Explain as fully as you can.

2 *Odd one out!*

1 Arch	6 Erosion	11 Notch
2 Abrasion	7 Freeze–thaw	12 Stack
3 Beach	8 Headland	13 Storm
4 Cave	9 Hydraulic action	14 Wave-cut platform
5 Cliff	10 Landform	15 Weathering

a) For each set below, decide which is the odd one out. Give a reason for your choice.

Set A	1	3	4	12
Set B	5	10	11	14
Set C	2	7	9	
Set D	6	8	13	

b) Make *two* sets of your own. Test them on your neighbour.

Key words

Abrasion – wearing away of rock by stones carried by waves
Freeze–thaw – frost action leading to the break-up of rock
Hydraulic action – wearing away of rock by the force of moving water
Notch – a small overhang at the base of a cliff
Storm – violent weather caused by strong winds, often accompanied by heavy rain
Weathering – breakdown of rocks by the weather

Can Britain's cliffs be stopped from crumbling?

>> **Understanding why cliffs are eroded at different speeds**
>> **Considering how to protect the coastline**

A The cliffs at Walton-on-the-Naze, Essex

B A close-up view of the cliffs at Walton-on-the-Naze

C The old sea wall at Scarborough

First of all, where are Britain's crumbling cliffs? The short answer is: 'in Lowland Britain'. The rocks found along the east coast of England are younger and softer than those in Highland Britain (see page 50). Soft rocks like those in photograph **A** are eroded quickly by waves. Why is the notice needed?

WHY ARE SOME CLIFFS ERODED FASTER THAN OTHERS?

The cliffs in photographs **A** and **B** are made of sandy rocks. They are not well cemented together, so the sand easily becomes loose. The cliff above soon collapses as waves wash against the cliff bottom. Look closely at photograph **B**. You can see that great chunks of cliff have recently moved. Look at the size of the area affected by cliff collapses. What shows that there has been recent cliff collapse?

CAN CLIFF COLLAPSE BE STOPPED?

The quick answers are both 'Yes' and 'No'. Obviously these answers are useless without some explanation!

Why is the answer 'Yes'?
Several methods of coastal defence are used to protect cliffs. The most common is a sea wall, which breaks the force of the waves before they can reach the cliffs. The old sea wall at Scarborough, Yorkshire (**C**) was built 100 years ago. What suggests that it is showing its age? Why do the cliffs behind it need to be defended against the waves?

New sea defences at Scarborough were urgently needed to keep the sea out. A major scheme of coastal protection, costing over £30 million for two kilometres of coast, was undertaken between 2002 and 2004 (photograph **D**).

- Great blocks of rock, called **rock armour**, were placed in front of the old sea wall in the bay.
- A new sea wall was built further out to sea around the headland.
- Large white concrete blocks were placed on top to protect it.

Why is the answer 'No'?

It would be far too expensive to protect all the English coastline that is at risk of erosion. Because Scarborough is a major seaside resort with shops, places of entertainment and homes, it was thought worth spending over £30 million to protect it.

Most cliff coastlines have farmland behind them, with just the occasional farmhouse and holiday home.

In the UK in 2002, building land cost on average 400 times as much as farmland. It costs from £5000 to build a metre of sea wall. Rock armour costs from £1000 per metre. On top of this, regular maintenance must be paid for.

So can the cost of coastal defences be justified outside towns? What might be the possible benefits of letting the sea back in?

D Coastal defence work at Scarborough in 2003: this part of the bay was a 'parking place' for the rock and concrete blocks to be used around the headland

Activities

1. Why are coastal defences expensive? Write down at least *three* reasons.

2. Make a frame. Draw a labelled sketch to show the physical and human features in **E**.

3. **Sea defences – for or against?**

   Divide into two groups, A and B.

   A meeting is going to be held in the village hall to decide whether to build sea defences in the area shown in **E**. Prepare a report to persuade people at the meeting to agree with your point of view.

   - Group A will represent the Local Authority in charge of sea defences. It is *against* spending money on sea defences

   - Group B will represent the farmer and the owners of holiday homes. They are *for* sea defences, and want them quickly.

   To help you prepare for this you can read about the struggle of local people at Mullion Cove in Cornwall. Go to www.heinemann.co.uk/hotlinks and enter the Express code **6437P**. Click on the link for Chapter 6, pages 82 and 83.

Key word

Rock armour – blocks of rock put in front of a cliff or sea wall to reduce the force of the waves

E Cliffs further south along the Yorkshire coast

Coastlines of deposition

>> Finding out about longshore drift and deposition

>> Understanding why beaches are important and need protection

What happens to all the rocks that are eroded from cliffs by waves? Waves remove them from the bottom of the cliff and transport them further along the coast. This process is called **longshore drift** (diagram **A**). While they are transported, the rocks are knocked about by the movement and are gradually reduced in size to shingle (small pebbles) and sand.

The sand and shingle are deposited elsewhere. This adds new land further along the coast. Waves take away from one stretch of coastline and give to another.

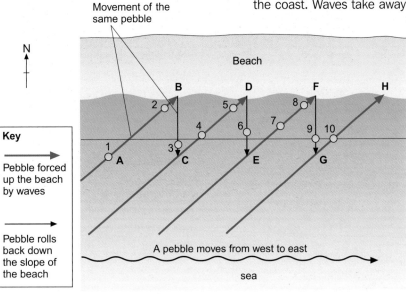

N

Movement of the same pebble

Beach

Key

→ Pebble forced up the beach by waves

→ Pebble rolls back down the slope of the beach

A pebble moves from west to east

sea

A Longshore drift: how sand and shingle are transported along a coast

WHERE DOES DEPOSITION TAKE PLACE?

Most **deposition** takes place where the coastline is sheltered, such as in **bays** (**B**). Bays are places where the coastline is set back, often in a large curve between two headlands. Sand is trapped in the shelter of the headlands and beaches form. Sometimes winds from the sea blow some of the sand on to land above the high-tide mark; this sand collects as **sand dunes**. You can see sand dunes beyond the beach at Bamburgh (photograph **A** on page 78).

At bends in the coastline, where the sea water is shallow, deposition may continue out into the sea. Long ridges of sand or shingle called **spits** can grow out from the beach, ending in the open sea.

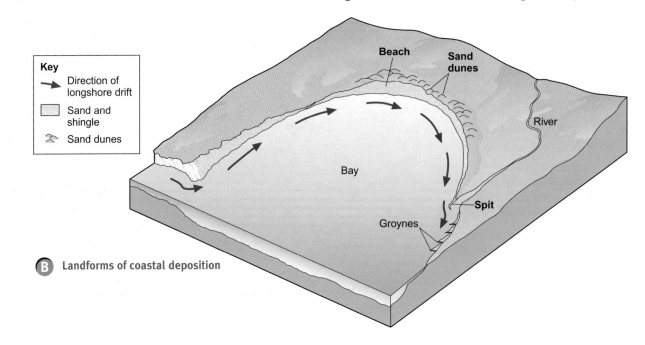

Key

→ Direction of longshore drift

▢ Sand and shingle

≈ Sand dunes

Beach

Sand dunes

River

Bay

Spit

Groynes

B Landforms of coastal deposition

WHY BEACHES ARE IMPORTANT

Mention the coast and what do people think about? Holidays? Spending the day on the beach? Swimming or surfing? For many people, the beach is one of nature's greatest landforms (**C** and **D**). Seaside resorts grow around the beach. The typical resort is long and thin as it hugs the coast behind the beach.

The beach is a seaside resort's greatest **economic asset**. What does this mean? Without it, fewer people would go there and less money would be spent in the resort. Therefore everything possible is done by local councils to stop beaches from being washed away during winter storms.

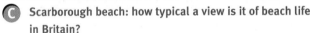 Scarborough beach: how typical a view is it of beach life in Britain?

D Eastbourne beach

Look at photograph **D**. Have you spotted these wooden posts and boards, or **groynes**, on the beach when you've been to the seaside? Groynes trap sand and shingle as they are moved along the coast by the waves. This makes the beach wider and deeper, so it is less likely to be removed by huge winter waves. Would there be a beach at Eastbourne without the groynes?

Activities

1. a) Why are groynes built?
   b) Write down *two* differences between groynes and sea walls.
2. a) Name the activities taking place on Scarborough beach (photograph **C**).
   b) What does the weather seem to be like at Scarborough on that day?
   c) State as many differences as you can between Scarborough and Eastbourne beaches.
   d) Which beach would you prefer to visit? Explain your choice.
3. **Class survey**
   a) Ask each member of the class to name what they would most like to do on a visit to the beach.
   b) Draw a graph to show the results. You can choose from any of the different types of graphs you have learnt about so far. (See pages 122 and 123 of *SKILLS in geography* for more help.)

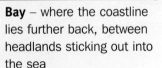

Key words

Bay – where the coastline lies further back, between headlands sticking out into the sea

Deposition – sand dropped by waves accumulating to form landforms

Economic asset – something that earns money for its owner

Groyne – barrier up and down the beach to trap sand and shingle

Longshore drift – movement of pebbles and sand along a coastline

Sand dune – pile of sand behind a beach

Spit – ridge of sand or shingle ending in the sea

Protecting Britain's great scenery

>> Learning about Britain's National Parks
>> Thinking about what National Park visitors can see and do

The UK is one of the world's most densely populated countries. It does not have large wilderness areas like those found in Antarctica (page 11). Natural landscapes need conservation and protection from the pressure of people. However, people should be able to visit and enjoy the wonderful British scenery wherever possible. Can you understand why it is hard to achieve the right balance between:

- allowing access for people
- preserving the natural beauty of places?

BRITAIN'S NATIONAL PARKS

In the 1950s the government chose ten areas of natural beauty and wild countryside to be **National Parks** (map **A**). They were created for two reasons:

1 **To preserve natural beauty:** by restricting new building and stopping the loss of more countryside (**B**).

2 **To provide opportunities for recreation:** by planning and providing footpaths, car parks and picnic sites for visitors to use (**C**).

An eleventh National Park, The Broads National Park, opened in 1989. The first National Park in Scotland, Loch Lomond and the Trossachs, was created in 2002, followed by The Cairngorms in 2003. The New Forest and South Downs in southern England will probably follow.

N

Cairngorms

Loch Lomond & the Trossachs

Northumberland

Lake District

North York Moors

Yorkshire Dales

Peak District

Snowdonia

The Broads

Pembrokeshire Coast

Brecon Beacons

Exmoor

South Downs

Dartmoor

New Forest

0   50 Miles

0   100 Kilometres

Key
- Old National Parks (1950s)
- New National Parks
- Future National Parks

A Britain's National Parks

 Mountainous areas

 Heather covered moorlands

 Wild uplands

 Dramatic coastlines

 Large lakes

 Underground caves

 River valleys and waterfalls

 Wildlife habitats (plants, animals and birds)

 Large forests

B Natural attractions of National Parks

Key words

National Park – a protected area of natural beauty and wild countryside

Recreation – activities done in free time and when on holiday

1 Make a larger version of this table. Using map **A**, fill it in.

National Parks in 2003			
	% of total area	**Number of Parks**	**Names of Parks**
England	8		
Wales	20		
Scotland	2		

2 Look at map **A**.

a) State where most of the original ten National Parks are located.

b) Write down *two* ways in which the locations of the new National Parks are different.

c) Where are the probable future National parks located?

3 a) Choose *one* National Park, perhaps the one closest to where you live.

b) Go to www.heinemann.co.uk/hotlinks and enter Express code **6437P**. Click on the link for Chapter 6, pages 86 and 87. Look at the Park website. Write down some of its main visitor attractions.

c) Plan a visit to the Park from your school.

(i) Show the best way to get there by planning the route from your school to the Park.

(ii) Plan a route that can be followed in the Park to include a selection of the main attractions.

4 Read newspaper report **D**.

a) Name the natural attractions in **B** that visitors to the Loch Lomond Park will be able to see.

b) (i) From the list in **C**, choose three possible activities for visitors to the Loch Lomond Park.

(ii) Explain why these activities are possible.

Walking and hiking   Rock climbing

Sailing and boating   Bird watching

Mountain biking   Potholing

 C Leisure activities of people in National Parks

Highland fling

Scotland gets its first National Park

The bonnie banks of Loch Lomond and surrounding areas were officially made into a National Park yesterday, the first in Scotland. It covers almost 30 000 square kilometres and includes some of the country's best scenery.

The Park contains 21 mountains, 33 hills, two forest parks and 57 sites of special conservation value for plants and animals. At its heart is Loch Lomond, the biggest freshwater lake in the British Isles, and an area rich in wildlife.

Scotland has come late to the idea of having National Parks, more than 50 years behind England and Wales. It has been worth waiting for. 'This wonderful area will now enjoy special protection and the funding that the National Park brings with it.'

D Adapted from an article by Kirsty Scott in *The Guardian*, 25 July 2002

Limestone scenery

>> **Finding out about Carboniferous limestone**
>> **Understanding how limestone produces distinctive landforms**

A Horton-in-Ribblesdale station, on the Settle to Carlisle railway line

B Limestone pavements are a distinctive landform

C Pen-y-ghent, one of the 'Three Peaks' in the Yorkshire Dales, seen from the railway station in Horton-in-Ribblesdale

Limestone produces landforms that are different from those of any other rock. They are an added natural attraction for visitors to the Yorkshire Dales and Peak District National Parks. Horton-in-Ribblesdale (**A**) is in the centre of limestone country in the Yorkshire Dales. For centuries local people have used limestone rock for building houses and dry stone walls (photograph **C**). Above the village are bare rock outcrops called **limestone pavements** (photograph **B**). These can only be found in areas of **Carboniferous limestone**.

Name of geological period	Millions of years	What was happening in the British Isles?
	0	Man evolved
QUATERNARY		Cool climate with warm intervals
	2	
TERTIARY		Mammals Birds — Clays and sands deposited in British seas and estuaries
	65	
CRETACEOUS		Reptiles and flowering plants — Warm climate, chalk formed
	140	
JURASSIC		Dinosaurs ruled the land — Warm wet climate, soft limestone formed
	195	
TRIASSIC		Bony fish
	230	
CARBONIFEROUS		Amphibians and insects — Shallow tropical seas, warm wet climate, dense forests from which coal formed, limestone and sandstone formed
	345	

D Part of the geological time-scale – you have probably heard of the Jurassic

WHAT IS CARBONIFEROUS LIMESTONE?

The geological time period between 350 and 285 million years ago is called the Carboniferous era (**D**). At that time, much of Europe was covered by a shallow, warm, tropical sea. The tropical sea was full of a great variety of marine life.

- When creatures died, countless billions of their skeletons sank to the bottom of the sea.

- Over millions of years they built up and formed thick sediments of almost pure calcium carbonate.

- Later this was compressed to form the hard rock that we now call limestone.

- Earth movements lifted the rock from the sea bed into mountain ranges on land.

WHY CARBONIFEROUS LIMESTONE IS SPECIAL

Carboniferous limestone is special because it forms distinctive landforms. There are two main reasons for this.

1 The rock is full of cracks

Brick wall shading is usually used to show Carboniferous limestone, because the rock is full of cracks (diagram **E**). Vertical cracks are **joints** and horizontal cracks are **bedding planes**. Both are lines of weakness that can be attacked by weathering, such as freeze–thaw. These joints and bedding planes make up the features of limestone pavements (photograph **B**).

2 It dissolves in rain water

This is an example of another type of weathering, known as **chemical weathering** (see **E**).

Surface streams are mildly acidic. When they flow underground they dissolve away the sides of the **caves** and **caverns**, making them larger.

Surface streams are acidic because when rain water reacts with Carbon dioxide, it makes Carbonic acid:

$$H_2O \;+\; CO_2 \;\longrightarrow\; H_2CO_3$$

water   carbon   carbonic
dioxide   acid

Weathering attacks the weakness in limestone

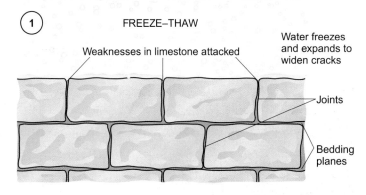

①   FREEZE–THAW

Weaknesses in limestone attacked

Water freezes and expands to widen cracks

Joints

Bedding planes

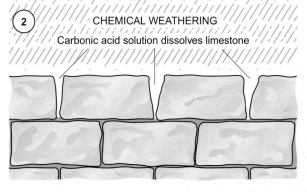

②   CHEMICAL WEATHERING
Carbonic acid solution dissolves limestone

E   The effects of weathering on limestone rocks

Activities

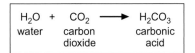   (S)

1   Draw labelled diagrams to show what blocks of Carboniferous limestone rock look like (see **B** and **E**).

2   Look at photograph **C**. Make a list of the physical and human features you can see.

3   a) Name *two* groups of people who might enjoy a visit to Horton-in-Ribblesdale.

     b) Explain why each group might enjoy going there.

4   Complete these sentences about Carboniferous limestone.

     A   Carboniferous limestone is made up of dead ...

     B   The skeletons built up to form ...

     C   Carboniferous limestone takes its name from ...

     D   The rock is full of cracks called ...

     E   Solution works on limestone rocks by ...

5   Make a table of the similarities and differences between freeze–thaw weathering (page 81) and limestone solution (chemical weathering).

Key words

Bedding plane – horizontal weakness between layers of rock

Carboniferous limestone – a grey rock made of calcium carbonate formed about 300 million years ago

Cave – small passage or hole underground

Cavern – large underground chamber

Chemical weathering – Carbonic acid in solution attacks the weakness in limestone and dissolves it

Joint – vertical crack within a layer of rock

Limestone pavement – surface blocks of bare rock

Carboniferous limestone landforms

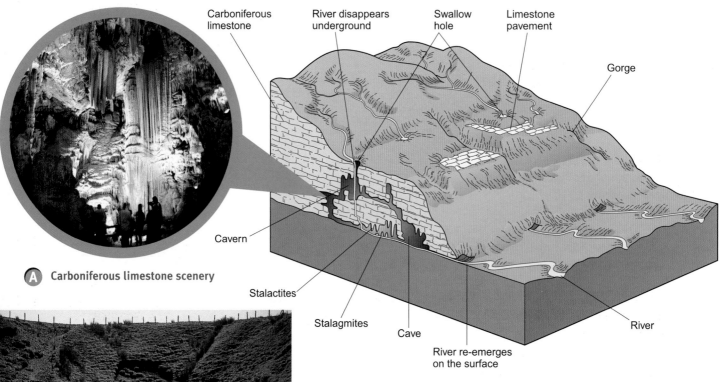

Carboniferous limestone

River disappears underground

Swallow hole

Limestone pavement

Gorge

Cavern

Stalactites

Stalagmites

Cave

River re-emerges on the surface

River

A Carboniferous limestone scenery

B Swallow hole at Gaping Gill

C Gorge at Gordale

Look at diagram **A**. Carboniferous limestone is unique in that distinctive features are formed under the ground as well as on the surface. There is a magical, but wet world underground that includes caves, caverns, **stalagmites** and **stalactites**. This underground world exists because the rock is **permeable** – it allows water through. In Carboniferous limestone country, surface streams disappear underground through the many joints and gaps in the rock.

RECOGNISING SURFACE LANDFORMS

Limestone pavements   You can see a limestone pavement in photograph **B** on page 88. These are bare rock outcrops, broken up into separate blocks. The flatter surfaces on top are called *clints*. The gaps between are *grykes*. Plants often grow out of the grykes.

Swallow hole   Below the large **swallow hole** (**B**) on the surface is a steep vertical drop underground. Surface streams disappear underground down these holes. Fell Beck disappears underground at Gaping Gill (**B**). Although the hole looks small and harmless, the vertical drop is 110 metres (350 feet)!

Gorge   A **gorge** is a narrow valley with rocky sides. In earlier times there may have been a roof over the top, which later collapsed. Can you imagine that the gorge at Gordale (**C**) was once a large cavern underground? Where could the pile of rocks have come from?

RECOGNISING UNDERGROUND FEATURES

Caves and caverns Underground, small passageways link together holes in the rock. Small holes form *caves*. Large holes, some of which open into great underground chambers, form *caverns*.

Stalactites and stalagmites Water with lime (calcium carbonate) in it drips from the roofs in caves and caverns. It forms **stalactites** that hang from the roof; they look like icicles, but are made of lime. Fatter columns of lime are built up from the floor; these are **stalagmites** (see **A** on page 90).

WHAT HAPPENS TO FELL BECK?

Map **D** shows the course of Fell Beck. A beck is a small stream.

- **Part I** – Rain falling on Ingleborough Hill feeds small streams that flow into Fell Beck. The rock on the surface here is impermeable – water cannot seep into it.

- **Part II** – When Fell Beck reaches limestone outcrops, it disappears underground down Gaping Gill (photographs **B** and **C**). It flows through a maze of underground passages and caves until it reaches the surface again through Ingleborough Cave.

- **Part III** – Back on the surface, Fell Beck is now called Clapham Beck, after the next village.

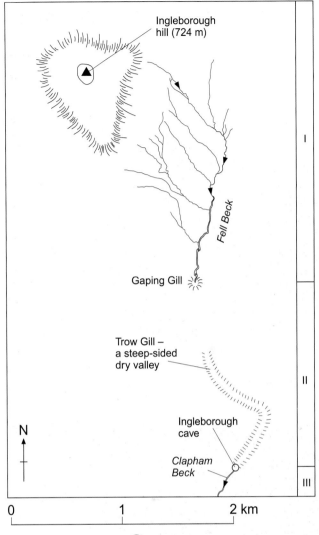

 D The route followed by Fell Beck

Activities

1 What is the difference between each of the following pairs?

    a) Permeable and impermeable rocks.

    b) Clints and grykes.

    c) Stalactites and stalagmites.

2 Look at photograph **B**.

    a) Draw and label a sketch of a swallow hole.

    b) What shows that many visitors go to Gaping Gill?

    c) Why do visitors to Gaping Gill need to take care?

3 ***What happens to Fell Beck?***

    a) Draw a sketch map to show the route followed by Fell Beck. Shade and label the three different parts.

    b) Explain why Trow Gill is a dry valley (no water flows down it).

    c) Ingleborough Cave is open to the public. Imagine you are a tour guide; prepare a commentary for visitors. For more information visit the Ingleborough Cave website. Go to www.heinemann.co.uk/hotlinks and enter Express code **6437P**. Click on the link for Chapter 6, pages 90 and 91.

Key words

Gorge – rocky steep-sided valley
Impermeable – not allowing liquids to get through
Permeable – allowing liquids to get through
Stalactite – 'icicle' of lime hanging down from a cave roof
Stalagmite – column of lime built up from a cave floor
Swallow hole – large hole down which a surface river disappears underground

Quarrying in the Yorkshire Dales National Park: good or bad?

>> Learning about quarrying in the Yorkshire Dales
>> Considering different points of view

Limestone has been quarried in the Yorkshire Dales for hundreds of years. Small local quarries were dug to provide the stone for building houses, churches, farm buildings, field barns and walls. There are more than 8000 km (5000 miles) of dry stone walls in the National Park.

Today only large quarries remain, like the one at Horton-in-Ribblesdale (**A**). **Quarrying** is big business. About five million tonnes of rock are quarried each year in the Yorkshire Dales. This is because limestone has many uses (**B**). Some uses are old; for example, famous London buildings made out of limestone include St Paul's Cathedral and the Houses of Parliament. Some are new; limestone is used in power stations to remove some of the harmful gases from burning coal.

(**A**) Horton-in-Ribblesdale quarry

ADVANTAGES AND DISADVANTAGES OF QUARRYING IN THE DALES

The obvious advantage is that quarrying provides jobs. The great demand for limestone makes quarrying a **profitable** activity. This is in an area where other types of work are in short supply. In some parts of the Dales the only other type of work available is farming, but it is hard to make a living from keeping sheep. However, tourism now provides new jobs in some villages.

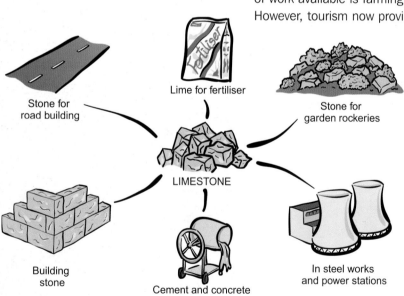

Stone for road building

Lime for fertiliser

Stone for garden rockeries

LIMESTONE

Building stone

Cement and concrete

In steel works and power stations

(**B**) Uses of limestone

There seem to be more disadvantages:

- Quarrying spoils the appearance of the countryside for visitors, and could mean fewer jobs in tourism.

- Noise and dust from the quarry are unpleasant for local people and visitors.

- Lorries cause traffic problems (**D**): nine lorries going to and from the quarry passed this point in Horton in a 20-minute period.

Are the advantages of quarrying greater than the disadvantages? It depends upon who you speak to. Even local people are often divided about whether quarrying is good or bad.

Key words

Profitable – money-making
Quarrying – removing rocks from the ground surface

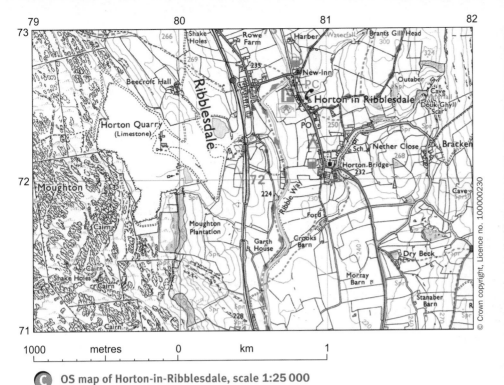

© Crown copyright, Licence no. 100000230

1000   metres   0   km   1

C   OS map of Horton-in-Ribblesdale, scale 1:25 000

D   Lorries in the centre of Horton-in-Ribblesdale – is there a problem?

Activities

1   Look at map **C**.

    a) Many tourists visit Horton. Draw *four* tourist symbols shown in the village. State what each one means.

    b) Name the long-distance footpath.

    c) Name the *two* other ways in which most tourists reach the village. State the map evidence.

2   a) Use map **C**. How big is Horton quarry? State its greatest length and width in metres.

    b) Work out its approximate area.

    c) Using photo **A** and map **C**, describe what Horton quarry looks like.

3   a) Look at photos **A** and **D**, and map **C**. What evidence is there for each of the three disadvantages of quarrying listed in the text?

    b) Explain why some local people like the quarry more than the tourists do.

4   Look at photograph **E**. It shows another problem that exists in all National Parks.

    a) Can you name the problem? What is the evidence for it?

    b) Suggest some ways of reducing the problem.

E   Near the summit of Ingleborough Hill

6 Great British scenery   **93**

Should there be more quarrying near Horton?

A An alum pit on the coast of Yorkshire

Stonedigger Quarries are seeking permission to open a new quarry near Horton. The district council are holding a public meeting in the village hall. Four groups of people will give their views at the meeting:

> **A: Local people from the village and surrounding area**
> **B: Managers of Stonedigger Quarries**
> **C: Members of the County Council**
> **D: Members of the Dales Tourist Board.**

1 a) Decide whether each group is going to speak FOR or AGAINST giving permission for the new quarry. Copy the line below. Then write letters A–D, representing the four groups, where you think they should go.

| Very Strongly FOR | Strongly FOR | Neither | Strongly AGAINST | Very Strongly AGAINST |

b) Say why you put the letters in these places.

2 Choose *one* of the groups.
a) Make a bullet point list of what the group might want to say at the meeting.
b) Put the ideas together into a speech to use at the meeting. You can get some ideas about quarrying in the Dales from the Internet. Go to www.heinemann.co.uk/hotlinks and enter the Express code **6437P**. Click on the link for Chapter 6, page 94.

3 Listen to, or read, the speeches of other class members representing other groups.
a) Draw another line like the one in activity 1. Put groups A–D on the new line. You may need to change where they go.
b) Say why you did or did not change where you put the groups.

4 Do you think the quarry should go ahead? Use the different views you've heard in activity 3 to explain your answer.

B Limestone quarry

>> 7 Shopping: past, present and future

In the Middle Ages most shopping or trading took place in market towns. There were stalls in the streets, similar to today's farmers' markets. Today the choice of ways to shop is huge and includes mail order and the Internet.

Learning objectives

What are you going to learn about in this chapter?

> The difference between convenience and comparison goods
> The pattern of shopping areas in a town in the UK
> What a shopping hierarchy is
> How to conduct a land-use survey
> What a sphere of influence is
> How to draw a flow line map
> How shopping has changed in the UK

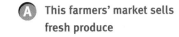

(A) This farmers' market sells fresh produce

(B) Shopping on the Internet

Where do people shop?

>> Learning about different ways of shopping
>> Understanding our pattern of shopping

A People buy cheap, everyday products at convenience stores like this

At the end of Chapter 3 you completed a simple shopping questionnaire to find out where people did their main weekly food shop. In this chapter you will investigate more about shops and shopping.

Geographers are interested in shops and shopping because they can see different patterns.

- City centres have a huge variety of shops, including very large stores such as department stores.
- Small settlements and housing areas tend to have very few shops, and these are quite small.

WHAT DO PEOPLE BUY?

People shop in different places for different items. Goods like bread, sweets and magazines do not cost very much. People do not travel very far to buy them. A family may buy everyday goods in convenient local shops such as a corner shop or newsagent's (**A**). These types of goods are called **convenience goods** or *low-order goods*.

B Shopping in the CBD, Newcastle upon Tyne

Clothes, shoes and furniture cost much more and people do not buy them as often. They also like to compare different brands and prices before they choose. These goods are called **comparison goods** or *high-order goods*. To have more choice, people travel to large supermarkets for their weekly food shopping. They travel even further, to the **CBD** of a town (**B**) or to an **out-of town-shopping centre**, to buy clothes. In the CBD there are many shops selling more expensive comparison goods such as clothes, shoes and jewellery.

Activities

1 a) Complete a shopping survey for your family by filling in a chart like **C**. If you can, fill it in for four weeks.

   (i) Which goods were bought most often?

   (ii) Which goods were bought least often?

Date of survey					
	Items bought	**Where we bought them**	**How we got there**	**Distance travelled**	**Approximate amount spent**
Monday	Crisps	Local shop	Walk	400 m	£1
Tuesday					

 Shopping survey

2 a) Make a frequency table like **D**. Choose *six* items that you and your family buy at least once a month.

   b) Draw a bar chart to show how many times you bought each type of item. Add another bar chart to show the distance travelled to buy each item. See SKILLS, page 00 for more help.

Items bought	Frequency – how many times you buy it per month	Distance travelled	Approximate amount spent
Paper/magazines	4		

D Shopping frequency chart

   c) Why do people:

   (i) buy some goods more often than others?

   (ii) travel greater distances to buy certain types of goods?

3 Make a copy of the chart below.

   a) Tick the boxes to show which are convenience goods and which are comparison goods.

   b) Now tick the boxes to show in which shopping areas you would find each item.

Items	Convenience goods	Comparison goods	Shopping area			
			Corner shop	Local shops	CBD	Out-of-town
Sofa						
Magazine						
Milk						
Fridge						
Ice-cream						
Trainers						
CD						

   c) Use your chart to say what types of goods are sold in each shopping area.

Key words

CBD – Central Business District

Comparison goods – more expensive goods bought less often, such as shoes, clothes and furniture. Also called *high-order goods*

Convenience goods – cheap, everyday items that are bought often, e.g. sweets, papers, bread, milk. Also called *low-order goods*

Out-of-town shopping centre – one or more shops built on the edges of towns and cities

A hierarchy of shopping areas

>> **Identifying a hierarchy of shops and services**
>> **Conducting a land-use survey**

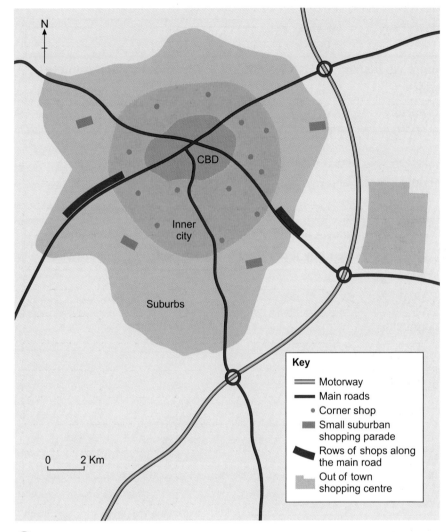

A Shopping areas in a UK town

In Chapter 2 you saw how settlements could be put into a **hierarchy** that showed their order of size or importance. Settlements can also be put into a hierarchy based upon the shops and services they offer. Large settlements such as cities have more and larger shops and services than smaller settlements. This is because they have a larger population to provide for.

Very small settlements, such as a single farm or a hamlet, may not have any services at all, or perhaps just a post box. A village may have a church, Post Office, public house and general store or newsagent. Towns and cities usually have a variety of shopping areas, including the CBD.

In a large town or city a shopping hierarchy (see map **A**) can be identified:

- many small corner shops, mostly located in the inner city area near terraced housing
- a few small shopping parades, often along main roads or in housing estates
- two or three larger suburban shopping areas
- the main shopping area in the CBD
- modern out-of-town shopping areas.

But how do we find out about a town's shopping hierarchy? To record shops and services accurately, geographers use a **land-use** survey (see **B**). The land uses can then be classified by type and the results used to make a land-use map.

Location:	Broad Street, Smalltown
Date and time:	30 September 2004
Weather:	Cloudy
Other comments:	Shops on main road, rather run down

Name of shop	Ground floor use	First floor use	Width of shop front (paces)
Wondertoys	Indoor toys	Kits and games	10

B Recording sheet for a land-use survey

1 a) Copy out the grid on the right. Tick the boxes where you think a shop or service will be found in the three settlements. Add up the total number of shops and services in each settlement.

   b) What do the results show about the size of a settlement and the number of shops and services it has? Give a reason for your answer.

2 a) Using the information in map **A**, count how many of each type of shopping area there are in the city. Complete a table like the one below.

Shopping area	Number
Out-of-town shopping area	
CBD	
Row of shops along main road	
Shopping precinct	
Corner shop	

   b) Describe what the table tells you about the numbers of different shopping areas in a city.

   c) Write out these sentences, selecting the correct word(s) from inside the brackets.

   A The CBD is (in the centre/on the outskirts) of a city.

   B The corner shops are (scattered/clustered) in the housing areas.

   C Most corner shops are (close to/far away from) the city centre.

   D The hypermarket is (on the edge/in the centre) of the city.

   E Shopping parades are found along the (motorway/main roads) leading to the city centre.

3 You are going to do some fieldwork. Visit a local area with some shops and services. Conduct a land-use survey using a chart like the one in **B**.

   a) Draw a bar chart to show how many examples of each land-use type you found.

   b) Describe what your graph shows. Can you explain the pattern?

Shops and services	Village (Population: 2000)	Small town (Population: 15 000)	City (Population: 100 000)
Large chain store, e.g. Boots			
Post Office			
Department store			
Bus station			
Primary school			
Cinema			
Public house			
Library			
Hospital			
Railway station			
Hairdresser			
Electrical shop			
University			
Supermarket			
Church			
Secondary school			
Government offices			
Newspaper printers			
Total			

Key words

Hierarchy – settlements put into order of size or importance

Land use – what the land is used for

How far do people travel?

>> **Understanding what a sphere of influence is**
>> **Drawing a flow map**

SKILLS

How to draw a flow map

1 Use a questionnaire to find where people have travelled from.
2 Show your results in a table like **A**.
3 Use a map showing the places named.
4 Look at the size of the values and the space on your map.
5 Decide on a suitable scale for the width of the lines, e.g. 1 mm for each person.
6 Work out the different line widths.
7 Plot lines of varying width from the shopping area to each place named.
8 Add a scale and title.

For more help see 0.0, page 00 of SKILLS.

Think about the shopping survey you completed on page 97. How far did you travel to buy a magazine or some sweets? How far did you travel to buy clothes, shoes or furniture?

Shops that sell comparison or high-order goods are usually in the CBD or an out-of-town shopping centre. These shops are expensive to run and need to have many customers to make a profit. A department store needs a very large **threshold population** to make a profit. A corner shop needs far fewer customers to make a profit so it has a small threshold population. It serves only the people who live close by, in local housing.

Village shops serve the village itself and surrounding farms. Large shops in city centres serve the population of the city and also people coming from other villages and towns. The area a shop serves is called the *catchment area* or **sphere of influence**. There are a variety of ways to find out the sphere of influence of a shop or settlement:

* a questionnaire asking shoppers how far they have travelled
* the delivery area of a shop or service
* the area that the local newspaper covers
* the catchment area of a local school.

Table **A** shows the results of a shopping survey held at a small retail park in Sunderland. This information was then presented in a flow map (**B**). This is a map which shows the sphere of influence of a settlement, that is, where people have travelled from to use a shop or service.

Where did you travel from?	Numbers of customers
Sunderland	18
Houghton-le-Spring	6
Washington	4
Durham	2
Total	30

A Questionnaire results at the Doxford Retail Park

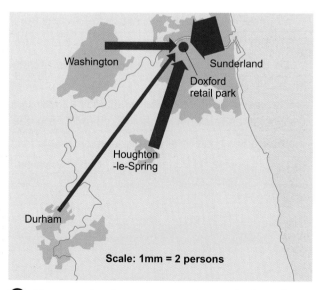

B Flow map showing customers using Doxford Retail Park

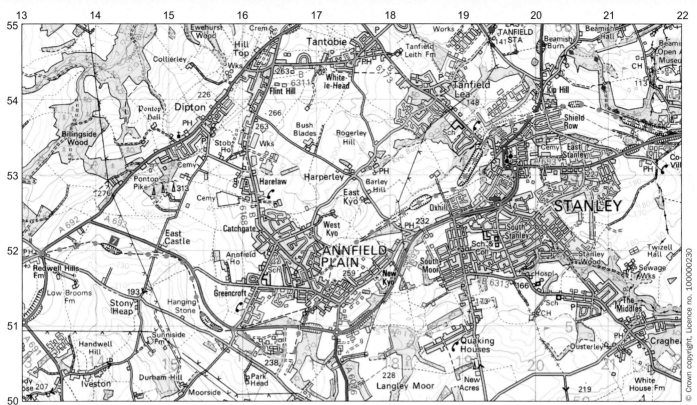

© Crown copyright, Licence no. 100000230

C OS map of part of NE England, scale 1:50 000

Activities

S

1 a) Place these shops in order of the distance you would travel to use them:

   post office   bakery   furniture shop   sweet shop   clothes shop

   b) Explain why you placed them in that order.

2 Study map **C**.

   a) Complete the table below to show which services are shown in each of the settlements.

   b) Fill in the final column to show whether you think each settlement is a single farm, hamlet, village or town.

   c) Which settlement would have the largest sphere of influence? Give reasons for your answer.

Key words

Flow map – a map that shows any kind of movement of people between places

Sphere of influence – the area a shop or settlement serves; also called the *catchment area*

Threshold population – the number of people a shop needs in its catchment area to make a profit

Settlement	Church	Post Office	Public House	Telephone	School	Cemetery	Hospital	Bus Station	College	Is it a farm, hamlet, village or town?
Annfield Plain										
Sunniside Farm										
Quaking Houses										
Stanley										
Tantobie										
Craghead										
Tanfield Lea										

How shopping has changed

>> **Learning how shopping has changed over the past 50 years**
>> **Understanding the features of out-of-town shopping centres**

Fifty years ago people shopped in corner shops close to their homes or travelled, often by bus, to town centres with many small shops, mostly privately owned. At that time there were no domestic freezers and few people owned even a fridge. Food went off quickly and had to be bought often – bread and milk usually every day. People's earnings were low and they were often paid weekly, so could not buy in bulk.

A The same chain stores are seen in most CBDs

As chains of stores, such as Boots and W H Smith, got larger they were able to offer a better range of goods at lower prices (**A**). Many small, privately owned shops went out of business. At the same time people were becoming more mobile. More people owned cars and could travel further to shop. Many people earned more and were paid monthly, so they could shop less often. Fridges and freezers became more widespread, and this, together with developments such as long-life milk and freeze-drying, meant that food could be kept longer.

In the 1970s, towns started to build brand new shopping centres in the CBD, often under cover. Chain stores were often grouped together under one roof (see the **Factfile C**). The first out-of-town shopping centre opened at Brent Cross, on the outskirts of London, in 1976, followed by many others.

Increasingly people shop without leaving their homes. Internet shopping and mail order, are both on the increase.

OUT-OF-TOWN SHOPPING

There are huge out-of-town shopping centres in many parts of the UK. They are all located close to very large centres of population. Can you think why?

Most out-of-town shopping centres are owned and run by developers. These large companies buy the land, build the shop units and then rent them out.

Today there is a lot of opposition to the building of more out-of-town centres. They may compete for business with the traditional CBDs and affect the environment. They are often built on farmland and they cause an increase in traffic.

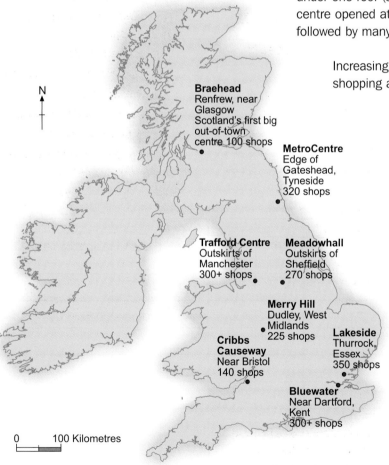

N

Braehead
Renfrew, near Glasgow
Scotland's first big out-of-town centre 100 shops

MetroCentre
Edge of Gateshead, Tyneside
320 shops

Trafford Centre
Outskirts of Manchester
300+ shops

Meadowhall
Outskirts of Sheffield
270 shops

Merry Hill
Dudley, West Midlands
225 shops

Cribbs Causeway
Near Bristol
140 shops

Lakeside
Thurrock, Essex
350 shops

Bluewater
Near Dartford, Kent
300+ shops

0   100 Kilometres

B Selected out-of-town shopping centres in the UK

But they are popular with developers, shop-owners and the public for several reasons:

- They use large areas of flat, relatively cheap land on the outskirts of cities.
- Rates and rents are usually lower than in a CBD.
- It is easy to build large single-storey shops.
- There is space for lots of free parking.
- They are usually close to a motorway network, giving easy access for deliveries and customers.
- The public prefer shopping 'under one roof'.

FACTFILE

Bluewater is an out-of-town shopping centre in Kent. It was built in 1999 on the site of an old chalk quarry.

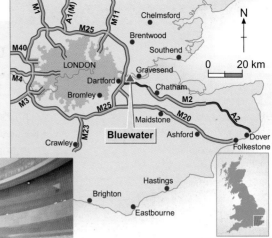

Bluewater:

- Cost £350 million to build.
- Has over 330 high-quality shops.
- Has 13 000 car parking spaces.
- Has over 40 cafés, bars and restaurants.
- Employs around 7000 people.

The centre includes:

- A thirteen-screen cinema.
- Six artificial lakes.
- A mini sports stadium.
- Homework clubs.
- Helpers available to talk over problems.
- Parkland to walk in nearby.
- A water garden with wildlife conservation project.

C Factfile: The Bluewater shopping experience

Activities

1. a) Describe the distribution of the largest out-of-town shopping centres in the UK.

   b) Suggest reasons for their locations.

2. a) Suggest *three* reasons why Bluewater was chosen as the site for an out-of-town shopping centre.

   b) (i) Give *three* features to be found inside the Bluewater centre.

      (ii) Give *three* features to be found outside the Bluewater centre.

   c) Write a paragraph describing what you could see and do at Bluewater. You can find more information on the Bluewater website. Click on www.heinemann.co.uk/hotlinks and enter express code **6437P**.

3. In pairs or small groups, discuss what the people below might think about shopping at Bluewater compared with in a CBD. What are the advantages and disadvantages for each of them? Present your findings in a class discussion.

   - An elderly person who does not drive
   - A mother with young children
   - A local resident
   - A shop owner in nearby Gravesend
   - A commuter who uses the M25 and A2 every day.

4. Using the Internet, research another of the out-of-town centres shown on **C**. Click on www.heinemann.co.uk/hotlinks and enter express code **6437P**. Use ICT to produce a leaflet or Powerpoint demonstration advertising the centre to local people. You could include a factfile, a photograph of the centre, a map of its location, and a list of advantages for the local area.

Shopping without leaving the house!

>> **Finding out how technology is changing the way we shop**
>> **Considering the pros and cons of Internet shopping**

Shopping from home using mail-order catalogues has always been popular, especially with the elderly and low-income families. Now there's another way to shop from home – Internet shopping. You can buy goods on the Internet from places all over the world. Anything from your weekly groceries to clothes, furniture and even cars can be delivered to your door. Do you think this will be the end of catalogue shopping (table **A**)? What will it do to traditional shopping areas in city centres and places like Bluewater?

	2001	**2006 (projected)**
Catalogue shopping	£9.7bn	£11.6bn
Internet shopping	£1.3bn	£14.4bn

A How shopping from home is changing

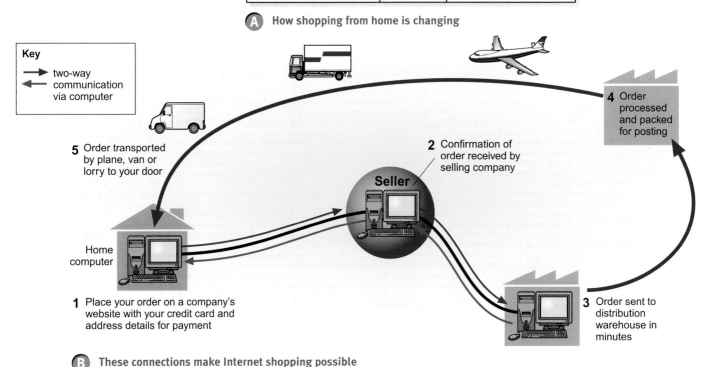

Key

→ two-way communication via computer
←

5 Order transported by plane, van or lorry to your door

Home computer

1 Place your order on a company's website with your credit card and address details for payment

Seller

2 Confirmation of order received by selling company

3 Order sent to distribution warehouse in minutes

4 Order processed and packed for posting

B These connections make Internet shopping possible

Figure **B** shows the connections that exist to make Internet shopping possible. So what are the benefits of Internet shopping?

- Anyone who has access to the Internet can use it to shop.
- You can buy things not available in the local area, even from abroad.
- Congestion and traffic pollution from shoppers are reduced.
- Shopping is easier for disabled people and those who live in remote areas such as the Scottish Highlands.
- Hassle-free – you can shop in the comfort of your own home.
- People selling on the Internet do not need to rent shop premises, so prices may be lower.

But are there any disadvantages?

- Some families, especially the elderly and those on low incomes, may not have Internet access.
- You lose the enjoyment of going shopping.
- The goods may not be exactly what you wanted – you can't touch them or try them on.
- It is expensive to return unwanted goods.
- Your credit card details may not be secure.
- Young people, the elderly and people on low incomes may not have credit cards.
- It may damage trade in shops, resulting in job losses.
- More delivery vans cause more congestion and pollution.

C Sainsbury's, delivering shopping ordered over the Internet

Activities

1. Look at **B**. Name *four* things that you know about the Internet and how it works.

2. a) Which of these items would you be happy to buy over the Internet? Give reasons for your answers.

   CDs   Designer trainers   Flowers   The weekly food shopping

   b) Design a questionnaire to find out what people in your family have bought over the Internet, and why. Contribute your results to a class activity to find out how much the Internet is used, and for what.

3. Imagine you are the managing director of a brand new computer software firm. You can sell your software *either* by setting up a chain of ten shops *or* by having one warehouse and selling it over the Internet.

   a) Which would cost less? Why?

   b) Which would give you the largest sphere of influence? Why?

4. a) Work in pairs. Rank the items below to show the impact you think Internet shopping would have on them. Start with the one that will be affected the most.

   - The local corner shop
   - Traffic congestion
   - A takeaway pizza business
   - A travel agent in a CBD
   - An out-of-town centre like Bluewater
   - A bank
   - Air pollution
   - Jobs in shops
   - Companies who deliver parcels

   b) Now work in a group. Compare your rankings and try to agree on a group ranking. Some items may have had the same ranking.

   c) Finally, discuss your rankings as a class. Produce a class ranking. In what ways is it different from your original ranking?

5. Suggest how Internet shopping might help:

   a) A family living in a remote area.

   b) A person who finds walking difficult.

   c) A young mother who works long hours.

6. Now suggest how Internet shopping might be a disadvantage for:

   a) A young person needing a new outfit for the next night.

   b) An elderly person with no computer.

   c) An immigrant family with no bank account.

Shopping: past, present and future

How and why has shopping changed in the UK?

People's age – we need people over 50 – Grandparents – neighbours?

How did they shop 50 years ago?

Convenience goods, e.g. bread, milk, papers?

Comparison goods, e.g. clothes, carpets?

Where did they go? How did they get there? How often?

How do they shop today? – for bread? – for clothes?

Where? transport? – how often?

Visit town centre? Or out-of-town centre?

 Notes on a class discussion

Title – How and why shopping has changed in the past 50 years

Introduction – why is shopping important?

Methodology – how you carried out your questionnaire survey and how you could have improved it.

Results – what the questionnaire showed – use graphs, maps, tables to show your information

Interpretation – describe how shopping has changed and why

Conclusion – summarise the main points

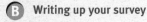 **Writing up your survey**

How shopping has changed – conducting a survey

You are going to do a piece of extended writing about how and why shopping has changed in the past 50 years. As part of your writing, include information you have collected from other people about how their shopping habits have changed.

1   Begin by brainstorming the idea with your classmates – what questions would you need to ask to find out this information? Agree on the questions and on who you need to ask. You can see the notes from a class discussion in **A**. Conduct your questionnaires for homework.

2   a) Use the answers to your questionnaires to sort out what the main changes have been and why they have taken place.
     b) Think about how good your questionnaire was – could it have been improved in any way?
     c) Consider the advantages and disadvantages of the changes in shopping that have taken place – consider different groups of people, e.g. the elderly, the busy career person, families with young children, and those who don't own a car or computer.

3   Plan and write up your findings – use the sub-headings in **B** to help you.

Internet shopping – an ICT investigation

4   You are going to investigate how and where to shop on the Internet.
     a) Think of a CD you would like to buy.
     b) Find two websites where the CD could be purchased. Click on www.heinemann.co.uk/hotlinks and insert express code **6437P**.
     c) Now compare the two websites:
       •   Were the prices the same?
       •   Which was easiest to use?
       •   Which gave the best information (for example, reviews of your CD)?
       •   Was there any difference in how you had to order and pay for the item (look at the delivery charges)?
     d) If you had the opportunity to buy your product on the Internet, which site would you use? Why?
     e) Print off a copy of the advertising material and order form for your CD from the website you liked the best. Hand it in with your answers.

» 8 Climate, people and future choices

Cambourne is a new settlement near Cambridge. Does it look like a good place to live? Is it going to be possible to house everyone who wants to live in the South East?

Learning objectives

What are you going to learn about in this chapter?

> The UK's climate and how it varies from one part of the country to another
> Where there are high and low densities of population in the UK
> Where it is planned to provide homes for more people in South East England
> Why new houses will be more welcome in some areas than in others
> Why keeping out the sea is becoming more difficult
> Whether the sea can be stopped

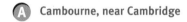

Cambourne, near Cambridge

What is the UK's climate like?

>> **Finding out about the UK's climate**
>> **Understanding how climate affects what people do**

To find out what the weather is like in the UK, you go outside or look out of the window (see page 9). To find out about the **climate** of the UK, you need to look at weather records for many years. When compared with other parts of the world, the British climate can be summarised as *cool* and *wet*.

WHERE IS RAINFALL HIGHEST?

Western areas are wetter than eastern areas (map **A**). There are two main reasons for this.

- **Prevailing** (most common) **winds** blow from the west. They have passed over the Atlantic Ocean and picked up moisture. By the time they reach land, they are wet winds.

- Most highland areas are in the west. Westerly winds are forced to climb over the mountains. This encourages the formation of cloud and rain. The lowlands east of the mountains are sheltered from the worst of the rain. The weather station with the highest rainfall in the UK is at Sty Head in the Lake District, with 3250 mm per year.

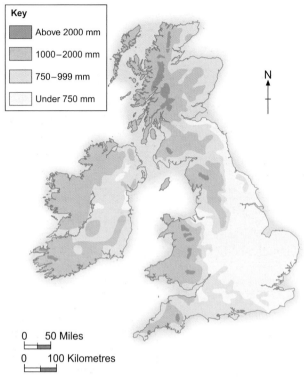

Key
- Above 2000 mm
- 1000–2000 mm
- 750–999 mm
- Under 750 mm

0   50 Miles
0   100 Kilometres

A Annual rainfall in the UK

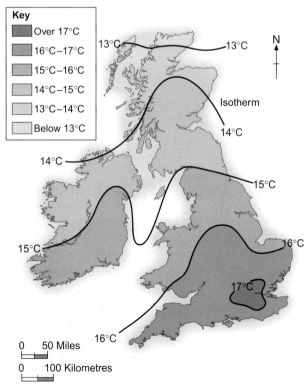

Key
- Over 17°C
- 16°C–17°C
- 15°C–16°C
- 14°C–15°C
- 13°C–14°C
- Below 13°C

13°C
13°C
Isotherm
14°C
14°C
15°C
14°C
15°C
16°C
17°C
16°C
16°C

0   50 Miles
0   100 Kilometres

B Summer temperatures in the UK (July)

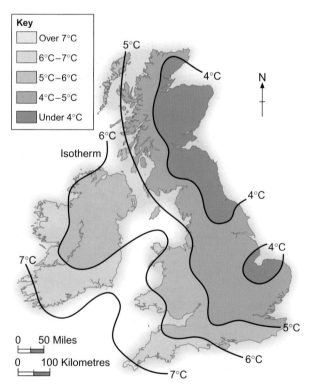

Key
- Over 7°C
- 6°C–7°C
- 5°C–6°C
- 4°C–5°C
- Under 4°C

5°C
4°C
6°C
Isotherm
7°C
4°C
4°C
5°C
6°C
7°C

0   50 Miles
0   100 Kilometres

C Winter temperatures in the UK (January)

WHAT IS THE CLIMATE IN THE UK?

Which is the warmest part of the UK in summer?

In summer, the south is warmer. The sunlight here is stronger because the sun shines from a higher angle in the sky. Map **B** shows this. The lines going across the map are **isotherms**. They join up places of equal temperature. They are used in the same way as contour lines on OS maps (see page 22).

Which is the warmest part of England in winter?

In winter, the west is warmer than the east (map **C**). Prevailing westerly winds have blown across the Atlantic Ocean, which in winter is warmer than the land. They carry some of this warmth on to the land, especially in the west. Heating by the sun is less important in winter.

Rain makes the grass grow well, and heavy rain on the mountains fills up **reservoirs** for water supply. Cereal crops such as wheat and barley prefer less rain and more sun. Knowing that the east is drier (map **A**) and warmer in summer (map **B**) helps you answer question 2 on map **D**.

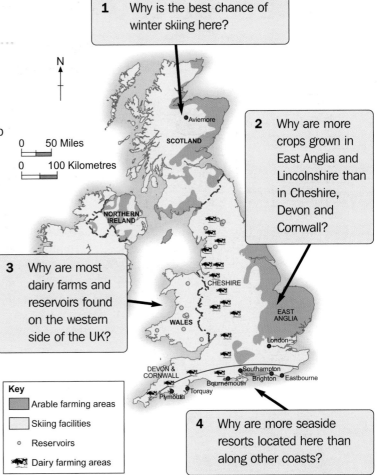

1 Why is the best chance of winter skiing here?

2 Why are more crops grown in East Anglia and Lincolnshire than in Cheshire, Devon and Cornwall?

3 Why are most dairy farms and reservoirs found on the western side of the UK?

4 Why are more seaside resorts located here than along other coasts?

Key
- Arable farming areas
- Skiing facilities
- ○ Reservoirs
- Dairy farming areas

D Activities affected by the UK's climate

Activities

Understanding the UK's climate will help you answer the questions on map **D** (use maps **A**–**D** to answer them). For example, you can answer question A if you know that rainfall is high in the west (map **A**).

1 Using information from maps **A** to **C**, write about the climate (rainfall and temperature) in your home area.

2 'Better climate' is one of the reasons people give for moving to south-east England. Is there evidence from maps **A** to **C** for a better climate in the South East? Explain what you think.

3 a) Cheshire is a well known type of cheese; Devon and Cornwall are famous for cream teas. Why?

    b) Give answers to questions 2 to 4 on map **D**.

Key words

Climate – the average weather conditions in a place over many years, such as temperature, rainfall and sunshine

Isotherm – line on a map joining up places with the same temperature

Prevailing wind – direction of the wind that blows most often

Reservoir – lake used for storing water for human use

Where do the people live?

>> Learning about density of population
>> Finding out why more people live in some places than others

The **average density of population** in the UK is 244 people per square kilometre, which is higher than for many other countries. This average, however, hides great differences in density. Some parts of the UK are almost empty of people, while others are very crowded. Map **A** shows the uneven spread of people within the UK. Where is the largest empty area?

Several large urban areas with high population densities stand out on map **A**. When a big city grows, it swallows up smaller towns and villages to form a **conurbation** – one large built-up area of houses, factories, offices and shops (see **C**).

If you put these large areas of high density from map **A** on a separate map, you will get a map of UK conurbations (map **B**). This map shows the most crowded places in the UK.

Why do more people live in some places than others? Some of the reasons (factors) are given in **D**.

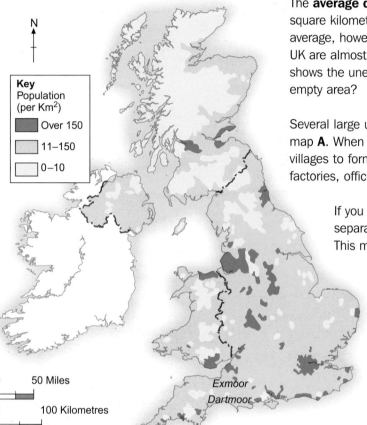

N

Key
Population
(per Km²)

	Over 150
	11–150
	0–10

0   50 Miles

0   100 Kilometres

Exmoor
Dartmoor

A Density of population in the UK

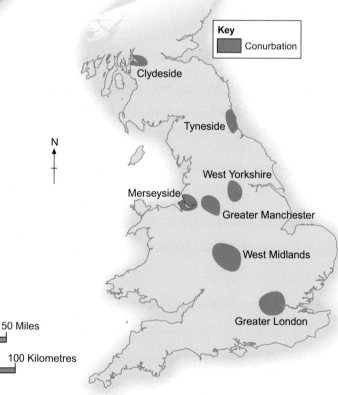

Key

Conurbation

N

Clydeside

Tyneside

West Yorkshire

Merseyside

Greater Manchester

West Midlands

Greater London

0   50 Miles

0   100 Kilometres

B The UK's big conurbations

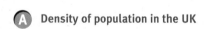

Key words

Average density of population – total population divided by the area

Conurbation – a large, continuously built-up area

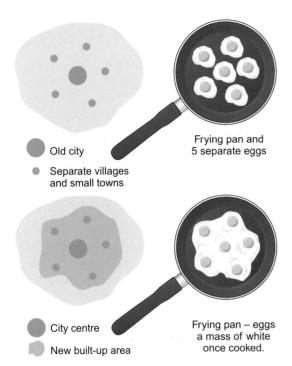

Old city

Separate villages and small towns

Frying pan and 5 separate eggs

City centre

New built-up area

Frying pan – eggs a mass of white once cooked.

C How city growth is like frying eggs

Factor	High densities of population	Low densities of population
Relief	• lowland • flat land Easy to build houses and roads	• highland • steep slopes
Climate	• warm • wet, but not too wet Good for farming and tourism More pleasant for people living there	• cold • high rainfall
Work	• many jobs • different types of work More ways of making a living	• few jobs • less chance of work

D Factors for high and low densities of population

Activities

1 a) Look at map **A**. How much do you agree with these two statements?

   A   Densities of population increase from north to south.

   B   Densities of population increase from west to east.

   b) Draw your own line of agreement like the one below.

   100% _____ 0%
   Agree   Do not agree

   c) Decide on your percentage of agreement for each of statements A and B. Show this by writing A and B on your line.

   d) Write a short paragraph giving reasons for your percentages of agreement.

2 Using information from **D**, draw two spider diagrams of reasons for high and low densities of population. Make clear which are physical reasons and which are human reasons (see page 6).

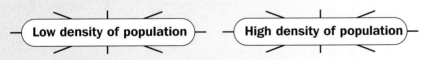

Low density of population   High density of population

3 Look at photographs **E** and **F**.

   a) Make a frame and draw a sketch of photograph **E** (see page 125). Add labels to show how and why population density is low.

   b) Make a frame and draw a sketch of photograph **F**. Add labels to show why population density is high.

   c) Make a list of the labels you used under two different headings – *physical* and *human*.

E In the Pennines (the upper Tees valley)

F The port town of Whitby

Can everybody be housed in South East England?

>> **Understanding why the South East is short of housing**
>> **Finding out about new growth areas in the South East**

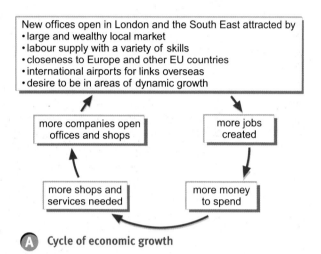

A Cycle of economic growth

The density of population in South East England is increasing. This is because people keep moving from North to South in the UK. Well paid jobs are more numerous in London and the South East than elsewhere (page 54). This is where today's fast moving economic growth is to be found. London and the South East are the engines pulling the rest of the country in the way that Manchester did during the Industrial Revolution (page 52).

Many new houses are needed in the South East. A government estimate is shown in **B**. How many extra homes will be needed over the next 20 years? How many new homes is that per year?

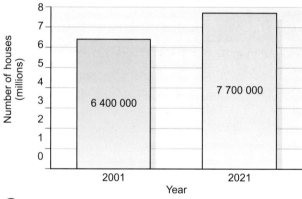

B Number of homes needed in London and the South East

WHERE ARE THE NEW HOMES GOING TO BE BUILT?

The government has plans for building new houses in the four main growth areas shown on map **C**. Thames Gateway is the area closest to the centre of London. Are all the growth areas close to motorways?

Some people are happy with the plans for Thames Gateway. This is because it is an example of a **brownfield site**. This means much of the land is derelict, and its *appearance* can only be improved by new building. Barking Reach (**D**) is part of Thames Gateway and plans for developing 80 000 houses there are underway. But, not everyone is convinced this is a good idea. Go to www.heinemann.co.uk/hotlinks and enter express code **6437P** to find out more.

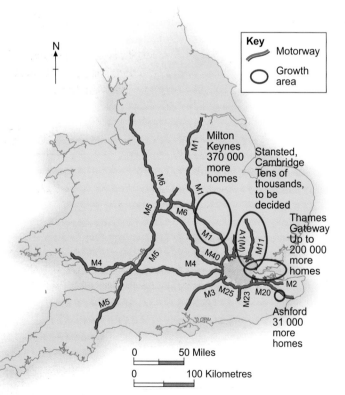

C Growth areas in the South East

BARKING REACH

Barking Reach in 2002

- It is located on a bend on the north bank of the River Thames.

- It was the site of an old power station and covers more than 100 hectares of polluted land.

- It lies between the Royal Docks and the old Ford car plant at Dagenham.

- On the banks of the Thames are derelict piers where barges used to dock.

- Some areas are used as illegal dumping grounds for everything from old cookers to cars.

Future plans

Barking Reach will be the largest example of brownfield or 'recycled' land in the country. Plans include:

- Building up to 15 000 new houses here (out of a total of 120 000 or more in Thames Gateway).

- Lining the banks of the Thames with riverside apartments and penthouses.

- Making a town centre of shops and cafés with tree-lined streets and a square with fountains.

- Extending the DLR (Docklands Light Railway) for a fast link into London.

D Part of Barking Reach: What shows that this is a brownfield site?

Key word

Brownfield site – previously built-up land that can be used again for new buildings

Activities

1 a) Look at graph **B**. How many extra homes are expected to be needed in London and the South East by 2021?

b) Make a table like the one below. Give it the title: 'Growth areas in the South East'. Complete it using information from map **C** for the other three growth areas.

Name of growth area	Location for London	Nearest motorway(s)	Number of new homes
Ashford	South east of London	M20	31 000

2 a) What is meant by a *brownfield* site?

b) List all the evidence you can find to show that Barking Reach is an example of one.

c) Why do planners prefer brownfield sites?

d) Draw a sketch to show how the area in **D** might look if the plans are carried out (see also page 125 of *SKILLS in geography*). Use the title: 'An artist's impression of Barking Reach in 2015'.

Taking a closer look at new settlements

>> **Finding out about two new settlements**

>> **Understanding local people's attitudes to the developments**

Key words

Business park – area of land laid out for offices

Greenfield site – land in countryside that is being built on for the first time

ASHFORD, KENT

Local opinion is strongly against building any more new houses in Ashford (**B** and **E**). There are two main reasons for this.

* The town has grown fast since 1990. Already 750 new homes are being built in Ashford every year – the new plans would greatly increase the numbers.

* Most of the new houses would have to be built on **greenfield sites**. Housing estates would replace green countryside.

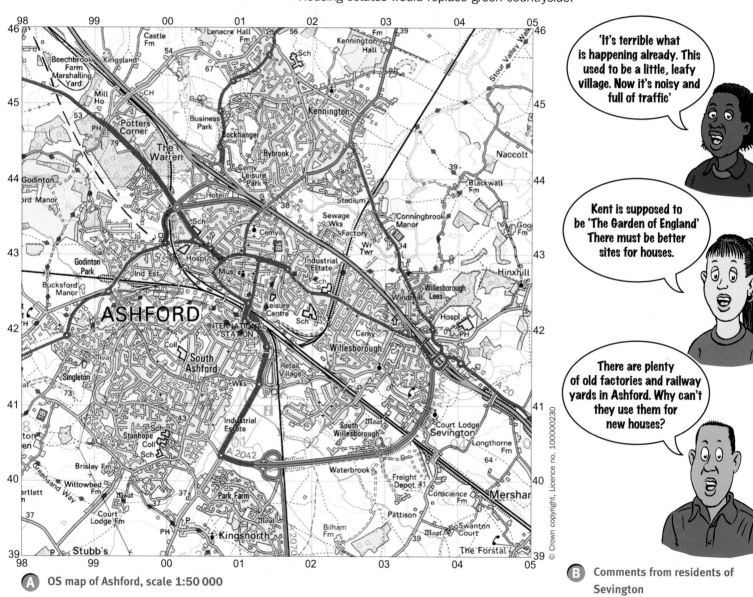

A OS map of Ashford, scale 1:50 000

'It's terrible what is happening already. This used to be a little, leafy village. Now it's noisy and full of traffic'

Kent is supposed to be 'The Garden of England' There must be better sites for houses.

There are plenty of old factories and railway yards in Ashford. Why can't they use them for new houses?

© Crown copyright, Licence no. 100000230

B Comments from residents of Sevington

Find Sevington on map **A** (square 0340). In 1990 it was a small village, totally surrounded by Kent countryside, and home to only 100 people. Today it is just another part of the built-up area of Ashford. New housing estates have filled the fields between Sevington and Ashford. Is there any countryside left around Sevington?

CAMBOURNE, NEAR CAMBRIDGE

Cambourne (**E**) is a brand new settlement situated nine miles west of Cambridge. It will become part of the Cambridge growth area (map **C** on page 112) and is planned to house up to 10 000 people. The builders bought the land from farmers. Building began in 1998 and was expected to last for at least ten years. You can keep up to date with its growth by visiting the Cambourne website. Click on www.heinemann.co.uk/hotlinks and enter express code **6437P**.

Included in the plans are:

- Homes of all sizes, from one-bedroom apartments to six-bedroom houses
- Services – shops, pubs, library, medical centre and schools
- Work – **business park** with jobs for over 5000 people.

A
Seventy-seven per cent of residents said they liked the design and layout of Cambourne.

B
Sixty-seven per cent said that they would like to stay.

C Summary of views from new Cambourne residents in 2003

D1 Around the green

D3 Supermarket

D2 Primary school

D4 Business Park

E Location map of Ashford and Camborne

D Views of Cambourne: do they suggest a high-quality environment for living?

Activities

1 Find the village of Kingsnorth (square 0039) on map **A**.

   a) Draw a large sketch of the village to show its site, layout and services (see also page 125 for more help).

   b) People in the village prefer to live here than in Ashford. Why? Write down as many reasons as you can.

2 Look at the nearby Park Farm housing estate. There are already more than 1500 homes on the estate.

   a) List all the differences you can find between Park Farm and Kingsnorth.

   b) Is Park Farm built on a greenfield or a brownfield site? Explain your answer.

   c) Assume that the plans for 30 000 new houses in the Ashford area go ahead.

   (i) What is likely to happen in this area around Ashford?

   (ii) Why might many local people object?

3 a) Draw two pie graphs to show what residents think about living in Cambourne (**C**). (See also page 122 for help.)

   b) Look at the photos in **D** and on page 107. Explain what has been done to make Cambourne an attractive place to live. You could use sketches to help you.

   c) Visit the Cambourne website – click on www.heinemann.co.uk/hotlinks and enter express code **6437P**. Find out *three* things about how much Cambourne has grown and changed.

Are people living in coastal areas of the UK safe from the sea?

>> **Finding out about rising sea levels**
>> **Drawing a line graph**

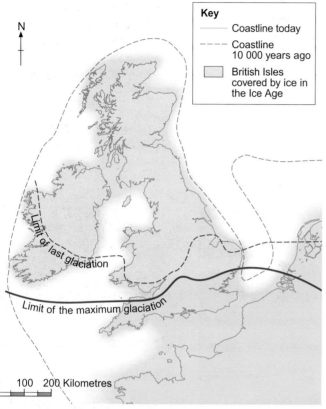

Key

— Coastline today

--- Coastline 10 000 years ago

☐ British Isles covered by ice in the Ice Age

N

Limit of last glaciation

Limit of the maximum glaciation

0   100   200 Kilometres

A The British Isles during the Ice Age

C Just a small Antarctic iceberg

Key word

Global warming – a rise in average world temperatures

While people living inland in South East England worry about population growth and building new houses, some people living in coastal areas worry about losing their homes. The UK's climate is warming up, especially in winter, and this is having an effect on sea levels. Consider these facts.

Fact 1: Sea levels are rising

Sea levels around Britain have been rising for the past 10 000 years. Map **A** shows the British Isles during the Ice Age, which ended about 10 000 years ago. Sea levels were 30 metres lower than today. The English Channel did not exist. People could walk to and from the Continent! At present the sea level is rising by 1–2 mm per year.

Fact 2: Average world temperatures are rising

People argue about whether the causes of **global warming** are natural or human. We do know for certain from temperature recordings that the Earth is warming up (**B**).

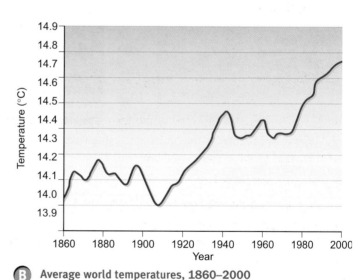

B Average world temperatures, 1860–2000

Fact 3: The world's ice sheets are melting

Ice in the Arctic and in Antarctica is becoming thinner. Giant icebergs keep breaking off, increasing the amount of water in the world's oceans and seas (**C**).

Fact 4: Cliffs are already crumbling

Some coastlines are already retreating (moving backwards), as you saw in Chapter 6 (page 82 in particular).

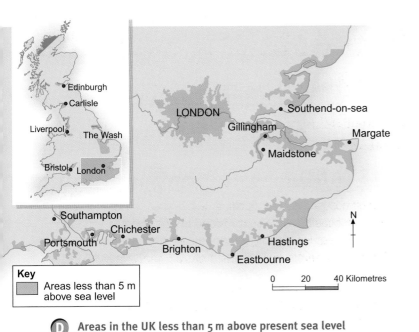

Key

| Areas less than 5 m above sea level |

D Areas in the UK less than 5 m above present sea level

Fact 5: There is a lot of low-lying land in the UK

The largest low-lying area is around the Wash (map **D** inset). Areas further south, in and around the mouth of the Thames, are close to areas of high population.

SKILLS

How to draw a line graph
1 Draw two axes, one vertical and one horizontal.
2 Label the axes for what is to be shown.
3 Look at the sizes of the values to be plotted.
4 Choose the scales and mark them on the axes.
5 Plot each value by a dot or cross.
6 Join up the dots or crosses with a line.

For more help see page 123 of *SKILLS in geography*

Fact 6: South East England is sinking

The UK is tipping like a see-saw. NW Scotland rises by 3 mm a year. It is still recovering from the weight of ice on top of it during the Ice Age. South East England sinks at the same time (**E**).

E The NW rises while the SE sinks

Activities

1 How was the UK different during the Ice Age? Write down as many differences as you can find.

2 Give the evidence for each of the following. Illustrate your answers with sketches and diagrams.

a) World temperatures are rising.

b) Cliffs are crumbling.

c) The risk from sea flooding in South East England is increasing.

3 You are going to draw a line graph (see the SKILLS box). Give it the title: *Total Emissions of Carbon Dioxide, 1860–2000.* Use the values in table **F**.

4 Read statements A–E.

A   Sea levels are rising.

B   Carbon dioxide emissions into the atmosphere are increasing.

C   People are to blame for global warming.

D   The Earth is warming up.

E   The number of big storms seems to be increasing.

a) Which of these five statements are facts?

b) Which are just opinions (people's views)?

c) What do you think the difference is between facts and opinions?

Date	Carbon dioxide emissions (billions of tonnes)
1860	25
1880	40
1900	60
1920	90
1940	125
1960	170
1980	275
2000	400

F Carbon dioxide emissions, 1860–2000

Can the sea be stopped?

>> **Recognising low-lying land on a map**
>> **Weighing up the options for coastal protection**

FLOODING AT CANVEY ISLAND

In January 1953 a big storm caused severe flooding in low-lying coasts in eastern England. Over 300 people lost their lives. Canvey Island on the Thames was one area that suffered badly from flooding. At the peak of the storm, water levels were 2 m above normal high-tide levels.

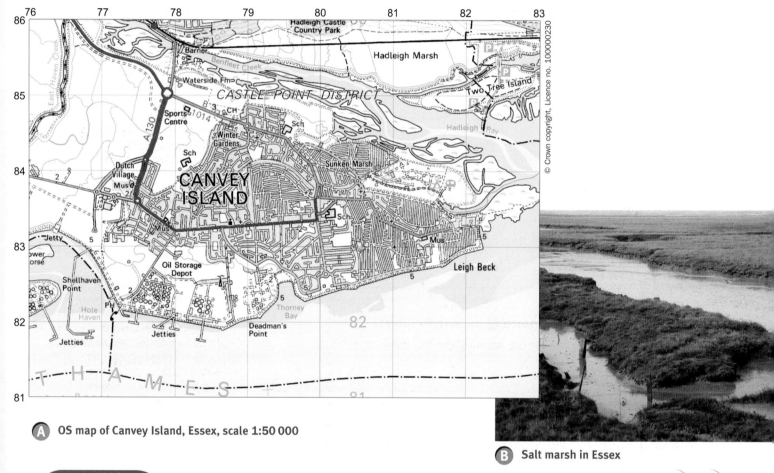

© Crown copyright, Licence no. 100000230

A OS map of Canvey Island, Essex, scale 1:50 000

B Salt marsh in Essex

Activities

Look at OS map **A** of Canvey Island.

1 Find the spot heights in square 7982. How many metres above sea level is Canvey Island?

2 Look at the names. List those that show that Canvey Island is a wet place.

3 On a sketch map of Canvey Island, show where the marshy and wet areas are found.

4 a) Give the four-figure reference of the square with the caravan and campsite in it.

   b) Would you be happy to use this site to park your new caravan? Explain your answer.

5 a) What shows that a lot of people live on Canvey Island?

   b) Name some of the places where they might work.

TWO OPTIONS FOR COASTAL PROTECTION

Option 1: 'Do nothing'

- Leave the coast to the forces of nature.

- When the waves destroy old sea defences, do not try to repair them. Let the sea invade and flood the fields, which will form salt marsh.

- Salt marsh vegetation will absorb a lot of wave energy as the tide flows in.

- Coastal birds will increase in number and variety.

- Accept the view that no matter what people do with the coastline, in the end nature will be the winner.

Is the salt marsh in **B** useful land or waste land? The answer depends on a person's point of view.

Option 2: 'Give the coast all the protection that is humanly possible'

- Build hard surfaces to stop the waves from reaching the cliffs. Examples of hard surfaces are sea walls and rock armour (pages 82 and 83).

- Build groynes out to sea to trap the sand and shingle (page 85).

- Keep the beach as wide and deep as possible.

A Owner of a farm on the coast
My father and grandfather worked hard to turn this land into fertile farmland. It is some of the best farmland in the country. Without new sea defences, all their work and mine will be wasted.

B Owner of a holiday home on the cliff top
My wife and I saved all our working lives. When we retired, we invested all our savings in this holiday home next to the sea. If our home is allowed to crash into the sea, we will be left with nothing.

D Council Treasurer
The cost of building and maintaining sea defences is great, and growing. We need to make sure that it is worth spending the money. There are many local services that need to be improved.

C Bird watcher
Every year two per cent more salt marsh is lost. The bird population has been falling for years as natural habitats like coastal marshes are lost.

E Economist
We no longer need to use all our farmland for food. The European Commission (EC) is already paying farmers for not planting crops on some of their land (this is called set-aside). It is cheaper for us to import many of the foods we eat.

Activities

1 **Should money be spent protecting the coast of Essex?**

a) Draw a line like the one below, showing the two different views about coastal protection.

_____ **A**

Spend no more money on sea defences   **Spend as much as possible to protect the coast**

b) Read the views of the five people given in **C**. The letter for farmer A has been added to the line. Mark the letters B to E where you think they should go along this line.

c) (i) What is your own view? Mark X on the line to show your view about protecting the coast.

   (ii) What is likely to be the view of people living on Canvey Island? Mark Y on the line.

   (iii) Explain why you chose points X and Y on the line.

d) Write a paragraph that begins: 'Different people have different views about protecting the coast of Britain because ...'

C What people think about protecting the coast of Essex

Climate, people and future choices

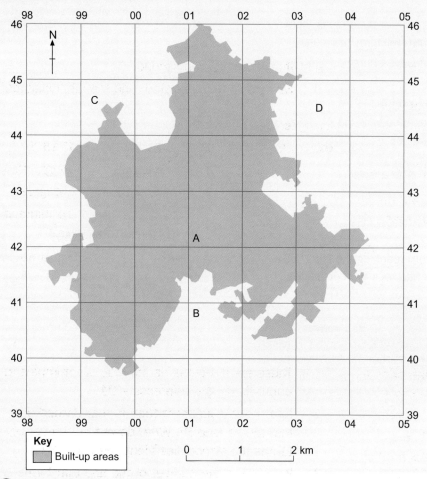

A The built-up area of Ashford in 2003

Finding land for new homes in Ashford

1 Look at map **A**. Letters A to D show four areas with space for new houses. Go back to the OS map of Ashford on page 114. Find areas A to D using the grid squares.

  a) For each area:

    (i) state how the land is being used and what it is like

    (ii) write down advantages and disadvantages for building new homes there.

  b) Which area is the best for new homes? Explain your view.

  c) Which area is least good? Why?

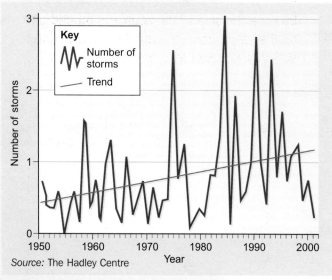

Source: The Hadley Centre

B Number of storms in the UK in January to March, 1950–2000

Stormy weather in the UK is increasing?

1 How does graph **B** show that stormy weather is increasing? Write down all the different ways that the graph shows this.

2 Go back to the OS map of Canvey Island on page 118. Draw another sketch map of Canvey Island. Shade on your map areas that would be flooded if a big storm increased water levels by 2.5 metres.

SKILLS in geography

1 ATLAS SKILLS

A How to use an atlas 1 – Countries of the world

1 Find the 'Contents' page in the front of your atlas.

2 Look for the heading 'World maps'.

3 Then search for a world 'political map'.

B How to use an atlas 2 – Finding a place

1 Turn to the 'Index' at the back of your atlas.

2 Places are named in alphabetical order.

3 The page for the map you need is given first.

4 Its square is given second.

5 Next its latitude is stated, and then its longitude.

Example:

Oxford, UK	5	5E	51° 46′N	1° 15′W
	Page	Square	Latitude	Longitude
			51 degrees	1 degree
			46 minutes	15 minutes
			North	West

The amount of information given, and the order, varies from one atlas to another.

2 OS MAP SKILLS

A How to give a four-figure grid reference

1 Write down the number of the line that forms the left-hand side of the square – the easting – 31.

2 Write down the number of the line that forms the bottom of the square – the northing – 77.

3 Always write the numbers one after each other – do not add commas, hyphens, brackets or a space.

4 Write the number from along the bottom of the map first, then the number up the side – 3177.

B How to give a six-figure grid reference

1 Write down the numbers of the line that forms the left-hand side of the square – the easting.

These are the same as the first two numbers in a four-figure grid reference – 31.

2 Imagine the square is then further divided up into tenths (see B). Write down the number of tenths the symbol lies along the line – 319.

3 Write down the number of the line that forms the bottom of the square – the northing. This is the same as the second two numbers in a four-figure grid reference – 77.

4 Imagine the side of the square is divided into tenths. Write down the number of tenths the symbol lies upwards in the square – 774.

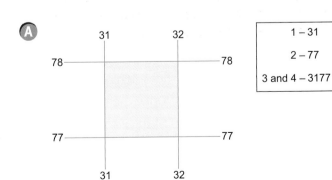

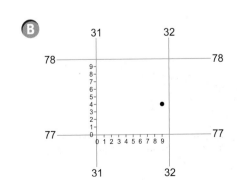

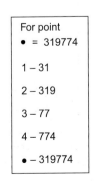

How to draw a cross-section

When drawing a cross-section from an OS map, you will need to find out the height of the land. See the example below.

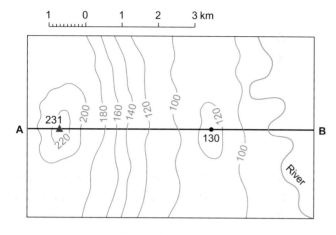

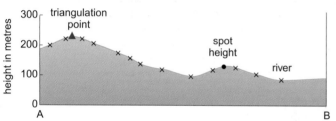

1   Place the straight edge of a piece of paper along the section and mark the start and end point of your section on the paper (AB).

2   Carefully mark on the paper the place where each contour line crosses. Note carefully the heights of the contour lines.

3   Mark on any interesting features, e.g. rivers, roads, spot heights.

4   Now draw a graph of your results. Draw a graph outline (see above). Note the lowest and highest contour height and use this to mark your y-axis (vertical axis) from 0 metres.

NB. Think carefully about the scale up the side – a good guide is 1 cm to 100 m for a 1:25 000 map.

5   Place your paper along the base of the graph and put small crosses on your graph at the correct heights and locations

6   Join the crosses together with a smooth curve – it is best to draw this freehand.

7   Add a title and labels for any key features, e.g. names of hills, rivers and roads.

3 GRAPHS THAT SHOW A TOTAL OF 100 PER CENT

This type of graph allows you to show the parts which make up a total. Think of using one of these four graph types whenever you have to present any data that has a total value of 100 (%). Graphs A–D all show the data in the table below.

Vehicle type	Number
Buses	20
Cars	70
Lorries	10
Total	100

A ten-minute traffic count near the centre of a UK city

B Pictograph

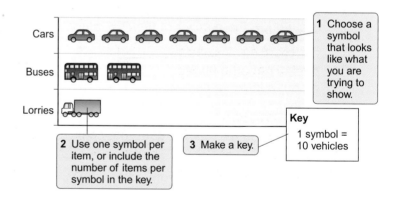

1 Choose a symbol that looks like what you are trying to show.

2 Use one symbol per item, or include the number of items per symbol in the key.

3 Make a key.

Key
1 symbol = 10 vehicles

A Divided bar graph

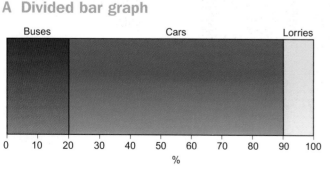

C Pie graph

1   If you need to, turn the figures you are using into percentages.

2   Draw a circle.

3   Start at the top (12 o'clock) and draw the segments (from largest to smallest).

4   Make a key.

D Block graph

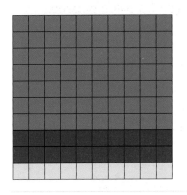

Key

- Cars
- Buses
- Lorries

1. Make a grid of 100 squares. Each square in the block shows 1 per cent.
2. Choose a different shade or colour for each value.
3. Shade or colour in the number of squares for the percentage.
4. Make a key.

4 GRAPHS

There are many different types of graphs. They are used all the time in geography. Sometimes it does not matter what type of graph you use. At other times, the type of data being shown needs a certain type of graph.

Always use a line graph to show **continuous data**. For example, the only way to show temperature is in a line graph:

J	F	M	A	M	J	J	A	S	O	N	D
4	5	7	10	13	16	18	17	15	11	8	5

Average monthly temperatures in London (°C)

A Line graph

1. Draw the two axes, one vertical and one horizontal.
2. Label what each axis shows.
3. Look at the size of the values to be plotted.
4. Choose the scales and mark them on the axes.

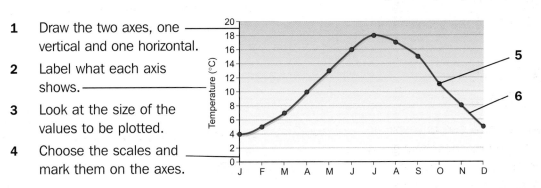

5. Plot the values by a dot or cross.
6. Join up the dots or crosses with a line.

B Vertical bar graph

This graph is useful for showing data that changes every month, or every year. For example, the best way to show rainfall is as follows.

J	F	M	A	M	J	J	A	S	O	N	D
54	40	37	37	46	45	57	59	49	57	64	48

Average monthly rainfall in London (mm)

1. Make a frame with two lines (called axes).
2. Label what each axis shows.
3. On the vertical axis (up the side) make a scale, large enough for the highest number.

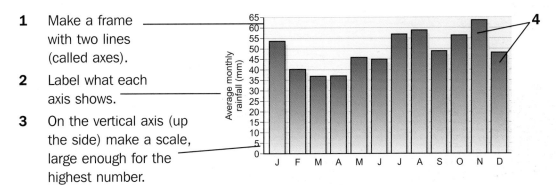

4. From the horizontal axis (along the bottom) draw bars of equal width.

3 OTHER TYPES OF MAPS

A How to draw a shading (choropleth) map

Shading (choropleth) maps show data for areas. If you have a table of data for named areas of the UK (or for anywhere else), it can be used to make a choropleth map (see page 54 Chapter 4).

1   Look at the highest and lowest values in your table of data, e.g. the highest and lowest wage.

2   Split the values up into four or five groups of equal size.

3   Choose a colour or type of shading for each group.

B How to draw a flow map

1   Use a base map showing the places named.

2   Look at the size of the values and the space on your map.

3   Decide on a suitable scale for the width of the lines, e.g. 1 mm for each person or 2 mm for every 5 people, according to the space available.

4   Work out the different line widths.

5   Plot lines of varying width from areas A, B and C to the town.

6   Add a scale to the Key and a title to your map.

C How to measure distances on a map

Using the cross-section map in 2C (page 122) and the instructions below, you can see that:

The distance between the spot height and the river along line A–B = 1 km

The distance between the trig point and the spot height along line A–B = 2.9 km

1   Using a piece of paper (or string if it is a winding distance) accurately mark the start and end point of the distance being measured.

2   Transfer the paper or string to the linear scale for the map.

4   Very important – always choose darker colours for the data groups with the highest amounts (values).

5   Look at your data to see which areas on the map match each value group you set up in step 2. Shade or colour in each area correctly.

6   Remember to add a key (see right)!

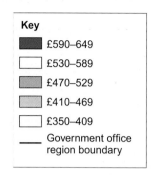

Key
■	£590–649
□	£530–589
▨	£470–529
▨	£410–469
□	£350–409
——	Government office region boundary

Table A

Where people travelled from	Number of workers
Place A	40
Place B	20
Place C	5

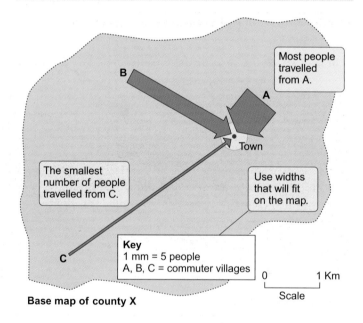

Most people travelled from A.

The smallest number of people travelled from C.

Use widths that will fit on the map.

Key
1 mm = 5 people
A, B, C = commuter villages

0 ———— 1 Km
Scale

Base map of county X

3   Put the left-hand mark on the zero and accurately mark the total number of kilometres on the paper.

4   Measure the bit that is left using the divided section of the scale. This will be in metres.

5   Add the two together to give the final distance measured.

6   Remember to give the units (kilometres or metres) in your answer.

6 SKETCHES

A Sketch map

The sketch map below was drawn from the OS map on page 15.
It was drawn to show differences in relief and drainage.

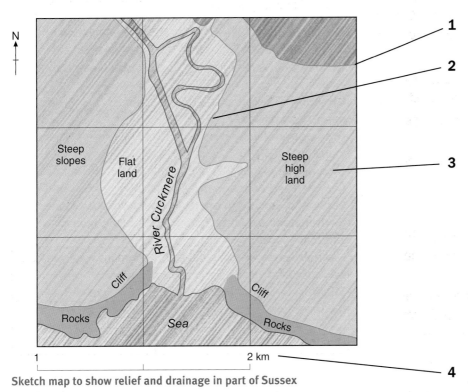

Sketch map to show relief and drainage in part of Sussex

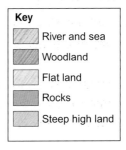

Key

	River and sea
	Woodland
	Flat land
	Rocks
	Steep high land

1 Draw a frame for your sketch map – think about its size and shape.

2 In pencil, sketch the features you wish to show. Start with some accurate major features such as a coastline or road, or even lightly mark on the gridlines and numbers.

3 Colour in your sketch map. Add a key for the symbols and colours you have used.

4 Add a title, north sign and scale.

B How to draw a labelled sketch from a photograph

Cley next the Sea, Norfolk

1 Make a frame the same size as the photograph.

2 In the frame, draw or trace the main features shown.

3 Label the main physical and human features.

4 Give your sketch a title.

Glossary

Abrasion Wearing away of rocks by stones carried by waves.

A-class road Main road built to link towns and cities.

Arch Rocky opening through a headland.

Atmosphere Layer of air surrounding the Earth's surface.

Average density of population Total population divided by the area.

Bay Where the coastline lies further back, between headlands sticking out into the sea.

Beach Area of deposited material (for example, sand and shingle) between the high and low tide marks.

Bedding plane Horizontal weakness between layers of rock.

Bird's eye view A view point from high above the landscape.

Brownfield site Previously built-up land that can be used again for new buildings.

Capital city The centre of government in a country.

Carboniferous limestone A grey rock made of calcium carbonate formed about 300 million years ago.

Cardinal points The main points on a compass: north, south, east and west.

Cave Hollow below the cliffs or a small passage or hole underground.

Cavern Large underground chamber.

Census Information collected by the government about people, such as how many people and where they live.

CBD (Central Business District) Zone of shops, offices and historic buildings, often in the centre of a town.

Chemical weathering Carbonic acid in solution attacks the weaknesses in limestone and dissolves it.

Cliff Steep rock outcrop along a coast.

Climate The average weather conditions in a place over many years, such as temperature, rainfall and sunshine.

Comparison goods More expensive goods bought less often, such as shoes, clothes and furniture. Also called *high-order goods*.

Congestion Too much traffic using the road at the same time.

Container A closed metal box for transporting goods by road, rail and sea.

Continent Area of land covering a large area of the Earth's surface.

Contour interval The difference in height in metres shown by two contour lines next to each other.

Contour lines Thin brown lines on maps that join together places at the same height above sea level.

Conurbation A large continuously built-up area.

Convenience goods Cheap, everyday items that are bought often, e.g. sweets, papers, bread, milk. Also called *low-order goods*.

Cross-section A diagram that shows the actual height and shape of the land, drawn as if the land has been cut in half.

Deposition Sand dropped by waves accumulating to form landforms.

Direction Uses the points of the compass to show the positions of places.

Drainage The natural water features, e.g. rivers, lakes and marshes

Eastings The lines that increase in value from left to right (west to east) on the map.

Economic To do with money, wealth or making money.

Environmental quality How good or bad a human landscape looks.

Environmental Affecting the natural surroundings (such as air, water, land, habitats and wildlife).

Equator 0° line of latitude around the middle of the Earth; the imaginary line dividing the northern from the southern hemisphere.

Erosion Wearing away of the Earth's surface by rivers, waves and ice.

Estuary Large mouth where a river goes into the sea.

Ferry Boat that carries people and goods over rivers and short sea crossings.

Fieldwork Work done in the area under study, out of the classroom and often out-of-doors.

Flow map A map that shows any kind of movement of people between places.

Freeze–thaw Frost action leading to the break-up of rock.

Freight Goods transported by water, land and air.

Global warming A rise in average world temperatures.

Globalisation Countries, people and companies are becoming more and more international.

Gorge Rocky steep-sided valley.

Greenfield site Land in countryside that is being built on for the first time.

Grid lines The blue lines that divide a map into grid squares that measure 1km squared.

Grid reference Used to locate either a grid square (four-figure) or a place within a grid square (six-figure).

Groyne Barrier up and down the beach to trap sand and shingle.

Headland Where rock extends further out to sea than the rocks on either side.

Heavy goods Bulky goods usually used by industries (such as coal, oil and rocks).

Hemisphere One half of the Earth.

Hierarchy Settlements put into order of size or importance.

Human geography Changes to the Earth's surface made by people.

Hydraulic action Wearing away of rock by the force of moving water.

Impermeable Not allowing liquids to get through.

Industrial Revolution Time of great factory growth from about 1750, based on using coal to make steam to drive new and bigger machinery.

Inner city Zone of industries and terraces built in the nineteenth century.

Island Area of land surrounded by water.

Isotherm Line on a map joining up places with the same temperature.

Joint Vertical crack within a layer of rock.

Land use What the land is used for, usually in zones in towns and cities.

Landform Physical feature of the Earth's surface.

Landscape The natural scenery of an area and what it looks like.

Lava Molten material that flows out of a volcano and cools into rock.

Limestone pavement Surface blocks of bare rock.

Lines of latitude Imaginary lines drawn around the Earth from east to west parallel with the Equator.

Lines of longitude Imaginary lines drawn around the Earth from north to south.

Logistics Organising the movement of goods (and sometimes people).

Longshore drift Movement of pebbles and sand along a coastline.

Manufactured goods Things that are made, usually in a factory.

Mental map Mental maps show images of what people think.

Motorway Road built to provide fast links between large cities and major centres of population.

Multi-national company One that has offices and factories in many countries.

Multi-national Including people from many different countries.

Multi-racial Including people from many racial groups.

National Park A protected area of natural beauty and wild countryside.

North sign An arrow that shows the direction of north on a map.

Northings The lines that increase in value from bottom to top (south to north) on the map.

Notch A small overhang at the base of a cliff.

Ocean Great body of water surrounding the Earth's land masses.

Out-of-town shopping centre One or more shops built on the edges of towns and cities.

Physical geography Natural features on the Earth's surface.

Polar regions Cold lands north and south of 60°.

Primary data Information collected by fieldwork.

Quarrying Removing rocks from the ground surface.

Raw materials Natural resources used for making other things.

Regional centre A large city, with many shops and offices, that serves the area around it.

Relief The height and shape of the land.

Reservoir Lake used for storing water for human use.

Rock armour Blocks of rock put in front of a cliff or sea wall to reduce the force of the waves.

Sand dune Pile of sand behind a beach.

Scale Converts the distance on the map to the accurate distance on the ground (tells you how long things are or how far apart they are).

Secondary data Information collected by someone else before you use it.

Service Something that provides for people's needs, e.g. a shop, hairdresser, doctor, school.

Settlement A place where people live, e.g. farm, village, town, city.

Site The physical land on which a settlement is built.

Siting factors Reasons for choosing a particular site for a settlement.

Sketch map A hand-drawn map, often a simpler version of another map.

Sphere of influence The area a shop or settlement serves; also called the *catchment area*.

Spit Ridge of sand or shingle ending in the sea.

Spot height A black dot where the height of the land has been measured. Often on a hill top or along a road.

Stack Pillar of rock surrounded by sea.

Stalactite 'Icicle' of lime hanging down from a cave roof.

Stalagmite Column of lime built up from a cave floor.

Suburbs Zone of housing estates built since 1920 on the outskirts of towns.

Swallow hole Large hole down which a surface river disappears underground.

Symbol A picture or drawing that represents real features on a landscape.

Temperate regions Lands between hot tropical and cold polar regions.

Terraced Houses joined together in a line.

Threshold population The number of people a shop needs in its catchment area to make a profit.

Triangulation pillar A concrete pillar once used in map-making, often on a hill top.

Tropic of Cancer Line of latitude $23\frac{1}{2}°$ north of the Equator.

Tropic of Capricorn Line of latitude $23\frac{1}{2}°$ south of the Equator.

Tropics Areas up to $23\frac{1}{2}°$ north and south of the Equator.

Trunk road Road built for heavy traffic.

Urban The larger settlements of towns and cities.

Wave-cut platform Gently sloping area of rock below the beach, seen only at low tide.

Weather Outdoor conditions at a particular time: hot or cold, clear or cloudy, wet or dry, windy or calm.

Weathering Breakdown of rocks by the weather.

Index